Nᵗʰ two different Designs for Candle Stands.

Act of Parliamᵗ 1761.

M Foster Sculp.

Furniture of the World

Furniture

of the World

Peter Philp

Octopus Books

First published 1974 by
Octopus Books Limited
59 Grosvenor Street, London W1

ISBN 0 7064 0146 8

© 1974 Octopus Books Limited

Produced by Mandarin Publishers
Limited
14 Westlands Road, Quarry Bay,
Hong Kong

Printed in Hong Kong

Contents

THE USE OF MATERIALS

Wood Of all the materials man has used for making furniture, wood has always been the most popular, in spite of the difficulties involved both in working it and in preserving it against the ravages of time and termites. Many other products, natural or manufactured, have been employed to embellish wood, and some have briefly challenged its supremacy. Nevertheless a widespread and deep-rooted preference for wood as a material constantly reasserts itself. Fashions for particular woods come and go, however, and vary not only from country to country, but also from region to region. Country craftsmen went on using certain timbers long after they had ceased to be fashionable in the cities, making out of solid oak, for instance, designs that were being executed in walnut or mahogany veneers by the master cabinetmakers in the great centres of production.

Veneering—the application of a thin sheet of decorative wood to the outside of a piece of furniture— is not necessarily a way of providing a poor article with a deceptively fine finish. True, it has sometimes been used to disguise shortcomings in the basic construction: in ancient Egypt, for example, the carcase was often built up with small pieces of wood jointed together, because large pieces were hard to come by, and the surface was then covered over with thin slices of ivory or ebony. Since the process was revived extensively in the seventeenth century, there have always been some makers who lavished their attention on the veneering of the exterior while caring nothing for the quality of the interior. At its best, however, veneering is a skilled and expensive process and the ability to practise it distinguishes the cabinetmaker from the joiner.

Veneers are simply thin slices of wood, and all those cut parallel to each other exhibit an almost identical figure in the grain. They can thus be reversed and matched up to make symmetrical patterns that would be virtually impossible in the solid wood. The veneers used to be glued to a carefully prepared solid surface by a lengthy and difficult process, until the invention of the modern machine method of veneering plywood made a much-maligned material available to the furniture manufacturer.

'Oyster' veneers, popular in the late seventeenth century, were cut across the grain of small branches, or sometimes the trunks of young trees such as laburnum, displaying the annual rings. Set side by side to form a kind of patchwork, they really do look rather like a dish of oysters. 'Burr' or 'burl' veneers were obtained by cutting across the grain near the roots of such trees as walnut and elm. Other finely figured woods such as mahogany and satinwood yielded beautiful veneers when the logs were sliced across at various carefully calculated angles. Oak, whether used in the solid or as veneer, exhibits its famous silver grain—pale, feathery markings—when riven lengthwise.

Different woods have often been used in combination by inlaying one into another of a contrasting colour. The earlier and cruder method was to inlay pieces of solid wood into hollows cut in a solid foundation. For example, sixteenth-century German chests of dark walnut were inlaid with designs in light-coloured woods such as box. Marquetry, developed in the seventeenth century, was the inlaying of a veneered ground with other veneers in different woods to make a pictorial design. Sheets of contrasting veneers, separated by sheets of paper, were lightly glued together before cutting the desired pattern through the entire thickness. When separated, the darker pieces could be fitted into the lighter, and vice versa. Each completed section of the jigsaw was held together by being glued to a sheet of paper, while the surface to be decorated was also given a thin coat of glue, which was allowed to cool. Then the marquetry design was laid down on it and a heated block of wood was clamped down over the marquetry, so that the heat melted the glue and caused the veneers to adhere to the carcase. Finally, the surface was sanded and smoothed, and additional effects were sometimes carried out with pen, ink and artificial stains.

Parquetry was the building up of geometric patterns —as distinct from the pictorial designs of marquetry— by laying small squares of contrasted veneers edge to edge. By skilful manipulation of colour and grain, an optical illusion of three-dimensional perspective could be created. One variation, which originated in Italy but was popularized at Tunbridge Wells in England, was to glue together a number of lengths of wood, undyed but strongly contrasted in colour, to form a

OPPOSITE
English cabinet made for the marriage of George Lawson and Margaret Trotter c. 1700. Dutch influence is evident in the shaping of the domed pediment and the marquetry decoration of birds and flowers in various woods and ivory on a ground of walnut veneer. The doors are crossbanded on the borders, the grain of the veneer running at right angles to that of the central areas.
BELOW
Detail of another cabinet, veneered in walnut with marquetry decoration in various woods; English, displaying Dutch influence, late 17th century.

RIGHT
Quartered veneers: four slices, cut from the same piece of wood, all exhibiting the same grain, assembled to form a symmetrical pattern.
BELOW RIGHT
Tunbridge marquetry: lengths of wood contrasted in colour were glued together to form a block from which slices were cut and assembled to form a continuous pattern.

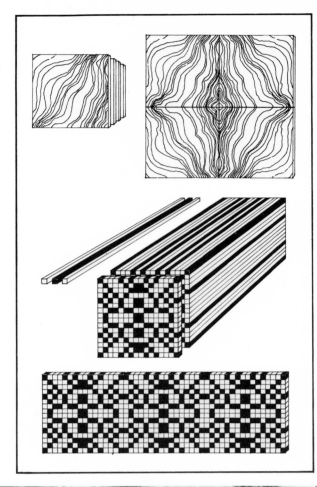

BELOW
Eighteenth-century French commode with parquetry decoration composed of small squares of veneer, their colours contrasting and their grains opposed to each other, creating a three-dimensional effect. This technique was used in many countries from the late 16th century.

solid block. It was known as Tunbridge ware. This was cut into thin slices, which could either be placed side by side to form a geometric pattern resembling parquetry or arranged to make a pictorial design as in marquetry.

The designs used for marquetry and parquetry have employed many subjects. Flower and plant forms were popular in the late seventeenth century. Delicate, leafy scrolls, symmetrically arranged, are known as 'seaweed' marquetry. From the sixteenth century onwards Italian tarsia or intarsia combined both pictorial and geometrical inlays to achieve remarkably vivid landscapes with buildings. A similar technique was employed in Germany. Floral and *chinoiserie* designs for the marquetry worker were produced by printmakers in eighteenth-century France. Between about 1770 and 1800 English cabinetmakers inlaid mahogany and satinwood with Neoclassical urns and figures.

A simple but effective use of contrasting veneers is to band the edge of a table top or a door with a wood of a colour different from that of the main surface, and with the grain running outwards towards the edge. This is known as 'cross-banding'. It is usually emphasized by a thin line of very light-coloured wood (or in some cases black) called 'stringing'.

All these are methods of enriching the outward appearance of a piece of furniture; they are not in themselves indicative of the quality within. This depends on the kind of wood used in such areas as drawer sides, where hardwoods such as oak are generally preferred to softwoods such as pine; although many excellent pieces of furniture will be found that are constructed entirely of softwood.

Metal One of the chief alternatives to wood as a constructional material for furniture is metal, and

various metals have also provided valuable accessories to wooden furniture (see pp. 12–13). It is perhaps significant that, while mention will be made of bronze chairs and tables in use in ancient Rome, the fine wrought iron of Spain, the cut steel of Russia, the brass bedsteads and cast iron tables with marble tops of nineteenth-century Britain and America, it was not until the early years of this century that the possibilities of tubular steel and, more recently, aluminium, came to be appreciated. Their importance today can hardly be exaggerated, especially in the field of furniture made for stacking in public rooms.

Plastics Following experience gained in World War II, American designers experimented with moulded plastics such as polyester reinforced with fibreglass for the bodies of chairs. In the 1960's an interesting range of furniture moulded entirely from plastics emerged, with Italy especially successful in producing new and attractive forms.

Glass Although glass was made by the ancient Egyptians and Syrians, and its decoration was carried to a fine art by the Romans, its use in furniture was delayed until about 1507, when mirror glass was first made successfully on the island of Murano, near Venice. A hundred years later, production was still limited to sheets of small size and these were very expensive. Then Venetian glassworkers risked severe penalties to leave Murano and sell its secrets, and with their aid, factories were successfully established in other countries. About 1680 technical improvements in French factories made the manufacture of large glass plates possible, but until about 1780 in many other countries mirrors more than about 2 ft (62 cm) long were frequently made up from two or three plates with the joins sometimes exposed or some-

LEFT
Door of English longcase ('grandfather') clock, c. 1685, the walnut ground decorated with marquetry in boxwood, in the 'seaweed' style, so-called because of the delicate tendrils of the design.

BELOW
French console table, c. 1740, with marble top on iron stand in the Rococo style. This was a relatively rare method of employing metal in the 18th century, when its use was usually limited to handles, mounts and other accessories.

times masked with strips of wood that matched the frames. Mirror frames generally exhibit the fashionable style of the period—Baroque, Rococo, Neoclassical—in its most extreme form, as they were hung on the wall and were less subject to damage than were most other articles of furniture. The woodcarver was therefore free to display his skill in elaborate and delicate sculpture.

'Toilet' or 'swing' mirrors for the dressing table, small enough for the plate to be in one piece, became popular in the late seventeenth century. In these the frame of the mirror is suspended between a pair of uprights which are often mounted on a base fitted with small drawers. Again, designs are consistent with contemporary fashions but in a much less extravagant way, carving seldom being employed. In the late eighteenth century full-length 'cheval' mirrors were produced with much the same swinging action as toilet mirrors, but standing on the floor and without drawers below. The usual shape was rectangular, but a circular type was made in France about 1800.

The mirror glass itself was decorated in several ways. Before 1700 a machine had been invented for bevelling the edges, originally to make it easier to fit them neatly into the rebate of the frame, but soon exploited as a decorative finish, which was sometimes heightened by cutting a design or by using strips of blue glass as a border. In *verre églomisé*—named after an eighteenth-century French designer who popularized, but did not invent, the technique—a design was traced on the back of the glass in gold or silver foil, set against a foundation of red, black or green. This form of decoration was particularly popular in America during the Federal period.

Mirror glass was used for glazing the doors of the bureau-cabinet—the American 'secretary desk'—of the William-and-Mary and Queen Anne periods. Although bookcases with clear glass panes divided by glazing bars are known to have been made in the 1660's, the practice did not become general until the middle of the eighteenth century. Few cabinet doors were made with single sheets of clear glass, without glazing bars, before 1800.

Porcelain This material was used by the Chinese in the Ming dynasty (1368–1644) for making headrests and, from the seventeenth century onwards, for tiles which were inset into chair backs and table tops. Faience tiles were used in many countries as splash backs for washstands in the nineteenth century. The earlier form of decoration was painting in blue under the glaze; early in the eighteenth century the painting began to employ a wide range of enamel colours over the glaze. In eighteenth- and nineteenth-century France the Sèvres porcelain factory supplied plaques for the decoration of cabinet doors, the friezes of writing tables and the tops of small tables. The method was imitated in other countries. In England Wedgwood's 'jasper ware'—which was not, in fact, porcelain but a very hard pottery—was used in much the same way.

ABOVE LEFT
Upper part and frame of a mirror of typical late 17th-century shape, decorated by the verre églomisé *method of tracing a design on the back of the glass against a coloured foundation.*

LEFT
Mirror with carved and gilded frame in the exaggerated Rococo style typical of Venice, mid 18th century, above a lacquered commode of the period.

RIGHT
French secretaire of the Louis XVI period, made by the distinguished ébéniste *Weisweiler and embellished with Sèvres porcelain plaques, costly to produce when new and now very expensive. Many good quality copies were made in the 19th century, and reproductions are still being made. The 18th century Sèvres porcelain was of a type called 'soft paste', different from the later 'hard paste' variety.*

Handles and other accessories

TOP ROW
Gothic and Renaissance:
15th century to early 17th century
a. *Turned and notched wooden knob;*
b. *Turned wooden knob with incised rings;*
c. *Iron triangular drop handle;*
d. *Iron ring handle with lobed backplate;*
e. *Iron shield-shaped escutcheon plate.*

CENTRE ROWS
Baroque:
Early 17th century to early 18th century
a. *Brass peardrop handle with star-shaped backplate, c. 1660–1700;*
b. *Peardrop handle shown in cross section with tang passing through drawer-front and secured with pins, c. 1660–1700;*
c. *Brass acorn drop handle, secured with tang, c. 1660–1700;*
d. *Brass escutcheon plate, c. 1660–1700;*
e. *Brass handle with pendant loop and engraved backplate, c. 1710–1730;*
f. *Miniature 'Dutch drop' handle used on small drawers and bearers, c. 1710–1760.*
g. *Brass escutcheon for cupboard door, c. 1730–1750;*
h. *Brass handle with pendant loop and fretted backplate, c. 1725–1740;*
i. *Brass escutcheon for drawer, c. 1730–1750;*
j. *Method of securing handle with nut and bolt, replacing tang method, c. 1710;*
k. *Brass loop handle discarding solid backplate in favour of pair of roses, c. 1750–1775.*

BOTTOM ROW
Rococo:
c. 1730–1760
a. *Escutcheon plate for door of armoire, steel or brass, c. 1740–1790;*
b. *Rigid, asymmetrical handle cast in bronze and gilded, c. 1740–1760;*
c. *Asymmetrical escutcheon plate, c. 1740–1760;*
d. *Traditional loop handle adapted to Rococo style, c. 1750;*
e. *Escutcheon for drawer of commode, transitional Rococo/Neoclassical style, c. 1760.*

Handles and other accessories During the late Gothic and Renaissance periods in Northern Europe the most common type of handle was a small, turned wooden knob. This was gradually replaced in popularity by a wrought iron ring, triangle or pendant drop suspended from a back-plate.

These types probably originated in Spain, where they continued in use long after brass had become the fashionable metal elsewhere. The popularity of brass dates from about 1650, but for the next 50 years much Italian and French furniture, though highly decorated in the Baroque style, was made without handles, the keys in the locks being made to serve the purpose. In Germany many pieces made as late as the nineteenth century were never fitted with handles. From about 1600 to 1700, both Holland and Britain favoured brass pear-drop or acorn handles, which were fixed by means of a 'tang'—a thin strip of brass that passed through a small hole at the top of the drop and through the thickness of the drawer-front, behind which the two ends were bent back and secured with small nails. This method was used early in the eighteenth

century on the first English and Dutch handles to have pendant loops; these had shaped backplates, sometimes with engraved decoration.

About 1710 nuts and bolts replaced the tang as a method of attaching the handle, and the one-piece backplate disappeared between about 1750 and 1775, during which time the loop was usually suspended instead from a pair of small brass discs or roses. The single backplate returned during the last quarter of the eighteenth century as a circle, oval or octagon embossed with Neoclassical motifs. A lion's head with suspended ring was also popular. This sequence of handles was common in England and America, and in those European countries where English influence was strong. Escutcheon plates to protect keyholes were regularly made to match.

After about 1715 in France and those countries which followed Parisian fashions, handles were made in finely chiselled ormolu—gilded bronze—which reached such a high level of artistic excellence that the designers were able to be especially sensitive to changes in fashion. During the transitional period between the Rococo and Neoclassical styles it was

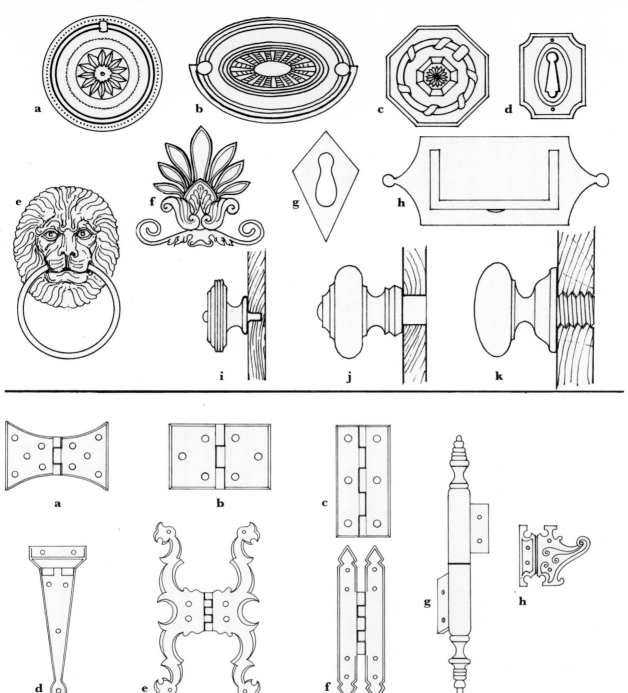

the bronze handles and mounts that first reflected the change. Mounts on the corners of commodes, for example, began as rather heavy, protective devices, but later became lighter and decorative rather than functional.

During the later Neoclassical phase which lasted from 1800 to 1825, small knobs of brass or wood came into use internationally, and the knob grew even heavier as the nineteenth century advanced. The traditional wooden knob had always continued in use in the rural areas of many countries, especially where strict sects such as the Shakers in America forbade the use of ornate brasswork. The Arts and Crafts Movement and the Art Nouveau enthusiasts of the later nineteenth and early twentieth centuries paid greater attention to metal mounts in hand-wrought iron and copper, the former favouring medieval styles and the latter adopting the sinuous line known as 'whiplash'. Since about 1920 the Art Deco and Modernist designers have tended to use handles which are formed as a straight bar, placed vertically, horizontally or diagonally, and made of either wood or metal, sometimes chromium plated.

Hinges Bronze hinges, replacing the strips of leather that had served more primitive civilizations, were used by the Egyptians as early as the Eighteenth Dynasty (1575–1315 BC). In medieval Europe the lids of chests were hinged on the outside with straps of iron, which were often finely wrought. In Britain the 'cock's head' and 'H' patterns were popular in the sixteenth and early seventeenth centuries, the common 'butt' and 'backflap' being made in brass as well as iron after about 1680. Between 1700 and 1800 it was the custom in France and neighbouring countries to use pin hinges, which enabled the heavy doors of armoires to be lifted off easily. In many rural areas a chest lid would be loosely hinged to the carcase by a pair of projecting pegs on the underside of the lid, which slotted into hollows cut into the back of the chest. This system, in use from ancient times until the nineteenth century, again enabled the lid to be lifted completely clear of the carcase. A similar principle was used in nineteenth-century French and German bookcases, in which the doors were fitted with pivot hinges so that they could be removed only by lifting the cornice.

Leather In the sixteenth century the finest European leatherwork was produced in Spain, mainly in the region of Cordoba. Elaborately tooled and coloured, and displaying a strong Islamic influence resulting from the Moorish occupation of Spain, it became famous all over Europe as *guadamecil*. After the middle of the seventeenth century, equally fine leatherwork came to be produced in the Low Countries. It was applied to chair frames, chests and screens with brass or iron nails. In Northern Europe plain cowhide was also used in the mid-seventeenth century for the seats and backs of chairs, to which it was nailed, often without any supporting upholstery. From about 1750 to 1780 leather in softer forms such as morocco was used, in combination with a webbing foundation and a stuffing of horsehair, for the seats of dining chairs in the English style. Leather then went out of fashion until the mid-nineteenth century, when it began to be used extensively on fully upholstered armchairs of the 'club' type, and button-backed 'Chesterfield' settees—the forerunners of much excellent modern seat furniture. Thin skins, known as 'skivers', were used from the eighteenth century onwards for leathering the tops of writing tables.

Papier-mâché This material originated in the East, and found its way to France and thence to Britain in the seventeenth century. In 1772 Henry Clay of Birmingham, England, patented a method of soaking sheets of paper in a mixture of glue and paste, pressing the sodden mass into moulds, drying it in a stove and finishing it off by dipping it in oil. Birmingham remained the chief centre into the nineteenth century for the production of boxes, trays, tables, chairs and even beds in papier-mâché, which were decorated with painting and inlaid mother-of-pearl. The best-known English makers were Jennens and Bettridge. By about 1850 similar work was being produced in the United States at Litchfield, Connecticut.

Stone Many primitive peoples used stone for ceremonial seats and altars, and in sophisticated societies it has been used since classical times, chiefly to form the tops of tables. Marble, used either in the solid or as a veneer, has been the most popular stone for this purpose, but many others have been employed to enrich it. In the sixteenth century Florence was the chief centre for mosaic work or *pietre dure*, a term applied both to flat surfaces in which a design of tiny coloured stones is bonded to a marble base with plaster, and also to arrangements of semi-precious stones set in relief onto a wooden base. In nineteenth-century Britain especially slate was also used for table tops, painted with floral subjects.

Plaster An Italian technique much imitated elsewhere in Europe in the late seventeenth and early eighteenth centuries was the overlaying of a wooden surface with a special kind of plaster called *gesso* which, when set hard, could be carved even more intricately than wood, and gilded. Another method of using plaster was to cast it in moulds and apply the castings to mirror frames and console tables—a method favoured in the nineteenth century for achieving a noble effect economically. *Scagliola* was an Italian substitute for *pietre dure* (see above) made by mixing small pieces of marble in a mixture of plaster and glue. *Stucco lustro* is plaster painted to simulate marble.

Varnishes and polishes Oil varnish—resin dissolved in linseed or poppy oil—was used in Northern Europe until about 1660, when a version made from lac and spirits of wine became more generally popular. Country-made pieces of furniture were usually oiled and polished with beeswax and turpentine. About 1820 'French polishing' with a pad soaked in a solution of shellac in spirit became popular in Europe and America. Much modern furniture is given a polished effect by spraying with cellulose or polyurethane.

BELOW
Nineteenth-century Spanish domed top travelling trunk covered in tooled leather, the shape and the Moorish style of decoration perpetuating a tradition established in the 17th century.

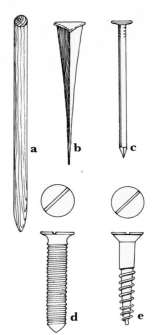

Nails and screws Iron nails of tapering shape, roughly square or triangular in section, have been used since the earliest times, but because they are susceptible to rust, much of the furniture made with them has fallen apart, whereas that in which the joints are secured with wooden dowel pins has tended to survive, thus giving rise to the fallacy that 'genuine antique' furniture is always devoid of nails. Wire nails of round section are a relatively modern development and their presence in a piece of antique furniture may be explained if legitimate repairs have been executed. After about 1600 hand-made screws of steel or brass with a short point and little or no taper began to be used in place of iron nails and wooden dowels. Machine-made screws with a pronounced taper have been made since the middle of the nineteenth century. Hand-made screws can usually be recognized even without removing them from the wood because the cut in which the screw-driver is inserted is hardly ever dead centre.

Textiles Upholstered seats were a rarity until the seventeenth century, and even then their use was confined to the rich. Very few seats, of any nationality, have survived from that early period with their original covering intact. The usual practice, dating from medieval times, was to soften hard wooden chairs by using cushions, which were often covered in needlework by the lady of the house. Italy established a textile industry in the sixteenth century and the expensive velvets of Genoa and the silks of Lucca commanded a world market. These crafts spread slowly northwards, with weavers from other countries settling in Britain about 1560 and producing wall hangings, drapes for beds and cushion covers. Early in the seventeenth century carpets began to be imported from Asia Minor into Europe, where they were ruthlessly cut up to upholster the seats of chairs. Imitations of carpeting were made, particularly in Holland and Britain, by drawing strands of wool through a linen backing to form a pile. Both the originals and the copies were known as 'Turkey work'.

In medieval times Flemish weavers had become renowned for their skill in weaving tapestries and in the 1660's some of them settled in Britain and helped to establish the famous factory at Mortlake in London. The Gobelins factory established by Louis XIV on the outskirts of Paris produced even more splendid tapestries and other upholstery fabrics,

in addition to manufacturing superb furniture for use in the royal palaces. Increasing persecution of the Huguenots in France brought the migration of many French weavers to Holland and Britain between 1685 and 1690, which greatly stimulated the textile industries in those countries. The eighteenth-century invention of the steam engine provided cheap power which made machine looms possible, and the nineteenth century saw an ever-increasing use of machine-woven fabrics on heavily upholstered chairs and settees. These textiles tended to follow traditional weaves and designs—velvets, brocades, plush, damasks—but more adventurous patterns began to appear late in the century under the influence of Art Nouveau. A material which became very popular in the 1930's was uncut moquette, which had a pile consisting of tiny loops and was often woven in patterns based on the Cubist Movement in art. At the same time a desire for simplicity began to find expression in the use of tweeds and corduroy as upholstery fabrics. During the second half of the twentieth century man-made fibres such as nylon have been blended with wool and cotton and treated with silicones, providing a wide range of hard-wearing upholstery fabrics.

LEFT
French settee, early 18th century, with a walnut frame upholstered in the original (but restored) tapestry. The Gobelins factory was established near Paris during the reign of Louis XIV to produce fine furniture and textiles, mainly for the royal palaces.

ABOVE
Fabric designed by William Morris. The firm of Morris, Marshall, Faulkner and Co was founded in London in 1861 with the aim of reforming the minor arts.

THE FURNITURE OF THE EAST

In most Eastern countries, furniture has changed so little over the centuries that it is difficult to integrate it into an account of furniture's development in the West. At various times, however, East and West have influenced each other considerably, and some knowledge of oriental types is desirable, both as a help towards understanding some aspects of Western styles, and for its own sake.

Chinese furniture can conveniently be divided into three main categories, according to the materials used: first, hardwoods—mostly types of rosewood, either native-grown or imported from Southeast Asia and Indonesia—sometimes inset with panels of porcelain, marble or woven grass; second, lacquer on a foundation of softwood, usually pine; third, bamboo—intended mainly for outdoor use in fine weather. Construction was chiefly dependent on the mortise and tenon joint and the dovetail, the corners being carefully mitred. Nails and screws were normally used only for affixing metal mounts. Most of the orthodox types of Chinese furniture were well established by the T'ang dynasty (AD 618–906), but the best extant examples were made between 1500 and 1800.

More than a thousand years ago, the Japanese were keen collectors of Chinese furniture, which was the original inspiration for much Japanese furniture design; but native genius brought about the creation of their own unique style. In Japan it is the custom to limit the number of pieces in any one room to very few, placed with a studied concern for spacing, the arrangement being frequently changed. Even the walls of the rooms are made to slide, so that nothing is permanent except the sense of lightness and grace.

An article peculiar to Japan is the kimono stand, which may look to the uneducated Western eye like a glorified towel rail, but is often a thing of great beauty, adorned with lacquer and engraved metal mounts. The sword stand—less an article of domestic furniture than a ritual object—was frequently decorated even more lavishly.

Japan was first opened up for trade with the West by the Portuguese in the sixteenth century but later closed her ports to all foreigners, with only the Dutch managing to retain a tiny but active trading post until the United States made contact in the second half of the nineteenth century. From then on there was a steady flow of Japanese artefacts to the West. The first organized display of Japanese lacquer in Europe, at the Paris Exhibition of 1867, greatly influenced design, and brought about a craze for Japanese styles, real or bogus, which reached its peak about 1880 with the 'Anglo-Japanese' furniture fostered by the designs of E. W. Godwin. These commercially produced designs, however, were debased by lack of understanding of the principles underlying oriental craftsmanship. Later in the nineteenth century, during the period of Art Nouveau, and early in the twentieth century, when oriental styles were studied afresh by the modern school, Japanese and Chinese designs had a more basic and pervasive influence.

The table The Chinese used a low table, originally placed on a platform called a *k'ang*, for reading and writing. Very low *k'ang* tables, with cabriole legs that terminated in square feet, were made as

early as the fifteenth century. Gradually, such tables came to be used on floor level, without the platform, and so were made rather higher, with straight legs which were often of round section—the shaping being executed by hand, without a lathe. Connecting rails united the legs a few inches below the top. Side tables were constructed on the trestle principle: a long slab of wood, sometimes with the ends carved to curl upwards, rested on end supports that in the simpler versions were slim, rounded legs, and in the more elaborate ones, slightly splayed legs united by panels of carved and pierced work in leafy, scrolled patterns. The Chinese did not set aside a special room for eating, so their meal tables were of portable size, either square or round and usually made to seat eight people, as a compliment to the Eight Immortals. If more than eight had to be accommodated, more tables were brought, and the company was split into groups.

Because it was customary in Japan to sit on the floor, tables there have always tended to be very low. Some are modelled on the Chinese *k'ang* table, while others are eight-lobed trays on cabriole feet.

In Persia, Turkey, Arabia and Morocco, small tables intended mainly for serving coffee, octagonal in shape and intricately inlaid with bone or carved with shallow, crisp designs, have long been a traditional feature of the bazaars. They formed an integral feature of the 'Turkish room', which was very popular in Europe during the latter part of the nineteenth century. Equally familiar in the West is the table that consists simply of a brass tray resting on a folding stand.

The chair Chinese hardwood chairs do not appear, at first glance, to be very comfortable but the square seats, of solid wood or even marble, were originally provided with cushions. The legs are usually straight and square with the corners slightly rounded, and are connected near ground level by understretchers, the front one projecting to provide a footrest. The basic squareness of the arms is

relieved by subtle curves, and the central splat of the back is often shaped to receive the human spine—a feature which was probably copied in the West from Chinese prototypes as early as 1700. Bamboo chairs with hooped backs provide a further concession to comfort. Decoration on hardwood chairs was achieved by formal carving of highly stylized symbols—dragons (regarded in China as benevolent) were a favourite subject. Chairs were made both with and without arms, the armchair being reserved, as in the West in early times, for people of importance. When in the presence of men,

ABOVE
*Miniature painting
depicting a side table
with upward-curving
ends, and a pair of low
tables or—more probably
—stools from which the
two women have risen.
Chinese, 18th century.*

LEFT
*Rectangular rosewood
table on square legs.
Chinese, 18th century.*

21

women usually sat on stools. Elaborate, thronelike chairs were made in lacquer.

In India, until the seventeenth century, the typical throne was very low, shaped like the lotus on which the Buddha traditionally sat. Thereafter it became a little higher and developed an octagonal shape, pinched in at the waist and richly carved and often lacquered. After the eighteenth century, as a result of the increasing trade with Europe, the Indian rulers acquired a taste for furniture in the Western style and had it made by their own craftsmen, often in rich materials. Chairs of European design were veneered in ivory.

In Islamic countries chairs with X-shaped frames, made to fold flat and inlaid with abstract designs or figures of birds, were known from very early times, but they seem to have been reserved exclusively for dignitaries and were unknown in the ordinary home, and little used even in that of the rich man, who preferred to sit on rugs and cushions placed on the floor.

The Dutch colonies founded in Indonesia in the seventeenth century produced a class of furniture known collectively as Batavian. The chairs were basically European in form but with their proportions curiously distorted, the legs turned and the backs carved in minute detail.

The bed Since the late seventeenth century, the Ottoman Empire has given its name to various kinds of sofas based on Western concepts of the Turkish couch. The word 'divan'—originally the name of the Turkish council of state, members of which sat on cushions raised on a low platform—has come to be applied to the modern divan bed in the West.

In India only the rich had beds, which were rather like modern Western divans in appearance. They rested on bell-shaped feet and were sometimes covered with canopies supported by posts of architectural form. Many antique Chinese beds also bear a resemblance to European four-posters. A solid platform with posts at each corner is almost completely closed by trellislike walls, surmounted by a canopy from which curtains hang.

The Japanese dispensed with all this, simply spreading a *tatami* mat of woven rushes on the floor, which would be enriched for the honoured guest by the addition of brocades to cover him while he slept.

The screen Although it originated in China, an important element in Japanese furnishing has always been the screen which, as well as acting as a draught excluder, provides another way of varying the shape of the room, and is itself often an outstanding work of art, its panels being lacquered and inlaid with shell, or painted on paper with stylized landscapes.

Lacquer Oriental lacquer is derived from the sap of a tree, *Rhus vernicifera*. The foundation of wood was first coated with unrefined lacquer and then allowed to dry before receiving successive further coats. Each of the first few was more highly refined than the previous one, and each was allowed to harden in a moist atmosphere before being rubbed down to a smooth finish, ready for the application of the next coat. Any number of coats between 16 and 30 might be applied, the final coat providing a glossy finish that could be decorated with gold powder. Alternatively, the entire surface could be carved—an art at which the Chinese excelled. Carved lacquer might be either of one colour, such as red (known in the West as 'cinnabar'), or a complex of colours built up by using lacquers of different hues for the succeeding coats; eventually, as the carver's chisel cut to the varying depths, this could provide multicoloured and three-dimensional designs. When the East India Companies opened up trade during the seventeenth century, this type became known in the

OPPOSITE
Revolving armchair, veneered in ivory, from Vizagapatam, India, 18th century. The shape is derived from a Dutch colonial burgomaster's chair, and demonstrates the way in which Indian craftsmen adapted European models for many pieces of furniture, decorating them by traditional Indian methods.

RIGHT
A bed of gilded wood, placed on an outside verandah, as depicted in a 17th-century Indian miniature painting which shows a lover leaving his beloved.
BELOW
Japanese lacquered leather screen depicting the arrival of Europeans. Lacquer was most often applied on a foundation of wood.

One of a pair of Chinese chairs with elaborately shaped backs. Such chairs are clearly intended as seats of honour rather than for comfort.

BELOW

Eighteenth-century oriental lacquered cabinet of the type exported to the West by the East India Companies. Cabinets of this type were made in both China and Japan, and decorated in gold on a black or coloured ground. This example stands on the floor, but it was customary in Europe, from the second half of the 17th century right through to the early 19th century, to mount such cabinets on stands which often bore no stylistic relationship to the subtle oriental workmanship.

West as 'Coromandel' lacquer or 'Bantam work'.

The Japanese produced lacquer in much the same way as the Chinese, though they refined it still further; they particularly excelled in surface decoration, filtering gold and silver dust through a bamboo tube onto a carefully prepared surface, achieving a variety of delicate finishes known to connoisseurs by their Japanese names, such as *togidashi*—rubbed-down gold and coloured lacquer.

The chest and the cabinet One of the most popular items of furniture exported from the Orient to Europe in the seventeenth century was the lacquered cabinet, fitted with a pair of doors enclosing many small drawers.

The Japanese chest of drawers was intended more as a container for precious manuscripts than for clothes, which in both China and Japan were usually stored in cupboards and boxlike chests with lids. The Japanese display cabinet usually had an asymmetrical arrangement of open shelves and small cupboards with hinged or sliding doors. Such cabinets would not be crammed with bric-à-brac, but used for the display of two or three carefully chosen objects of art, which were frequently changed for others kept in reserve.

In China storage cupboards were usually of hardwood, built on severe lines with no projecting mouldings, so that they could stand touching each other and be treated as interchangeable units—a principle further extended by placing small cupboards on top of the larger ones. Face hinges of engraved brass attached the doors to the carcase,

ABOVE

Chinese armchair, inlaid with mother-of-pearl, c. 1830. This style of decoration was also practised in Japan, where it became known as 'Shibayama work', after a family of craftsmen who excelled in it.

ABOVE
*Eighteenth-century
Korean marriage chest,
showing strong Japanese
influence in the decoration
of the metal mounts.
Korean furniture is often
mistaken for Chinese or
Japanese, as a
consequence of the
influence exerted on
Korean history and
culture by both China
and Japan at various
times. The concept of the
marriage chest was very
widespread in the East
and the West until the
nineteenth century, the
idea still being
perpetuated in the phrase,
spoken to a girl
anticipating marriage,
'something for your
bottom drawer'.*

and the style of engraving is often the best clue to dating these timeless pieces. Generally speaking, the more ornate the engraving, the more recent the article.

Korea, which has been subject to both China and Japan at various times in its history, was effectively closed to the West until the 1880's. When trade became possible, an interesting range of furniture was found to have evolved there, the medicine cabinet composed of many small drawers being one of the most distinctive types.

From the time of India's colonization by European countries, a quantity of furniture was made in the country for foreigners resident there, and also for export to the West. General shapes were usually based on European types, but the decoration was taken from Indian culture. The Portuguese colony of Goa, in particular, produced a distinctive form of cabinet of drawers, which was inlaid with abstract or floral designs in bone and mounted on a stand carved with representations of mermaids.

The Arabs, being largely nomadic, had little need of furniture, but chests with decorative designs in the Islamic style studded with brass-headed nails were used by traders for transporting valuables in their dhows, at least from medieval times until the present, and specimens—some of dubious antiquity—can still be bought in seaports East African coast.

THE SEQUENCE OF STYLES IN THE WEST

OPPOSITE
Detail from the inner side of the back of the throne of Tutankhamun, Pharaoh of Egypt about the middle of the 14th century BC. Made of gold inlaid with cornelian, lapis lazuli and rock crystal, this depicts the boy king seated on a typical throne, its legs carved to represent animals and fitted with a footrest. The table is also typical of a type which, like the chair, survived with little change in Egypt for about 2,000 years.

BELOW
Assyrian carved relief from the palace of King Assurbanipal (668–626 BC) at Nineveh, showing him banqueting with his queen. At this early date, such sophisticated pieces of furniture as the couch and the chair are shown in an advanced stage of development, the legs seemingly having been turned on a lathe.

The names applied to furniture styles are a little like flags of convenience on ships: useful for purposes of cursory identification, but sometimes misleading. Even the most sophisticated designers seldom abandoned one style completely when replacing it with another; almost always there has been a transitional phase between one dominant mood and the next. The unsophisticated craftsman in a country town might adopt a mannerism years—even decades—after it had ceased to be fashionable in the cities. Many designs which appeared in certain places at particular times have in fact been borrowed from other places and times—often from the remote past.

Classical beginnings As early as 1500 BC, the Egyptians had developed the bed, the chair, the chest and the table to a pitch of refinement that demanded a wide range of techniques and a variety of materials. Legs were carved to represent those of animals or, if plain and vertical, were braced with diagonal struts. The X-shaped support, which was to appear time and again in subsequent periods, was also used. Figurative and abstract decoration was painted or inlaid with ebony, ivory and semi-precious stones.

The Greeks adapted many Egyptian ideas in the process of evolving their own style, which can be clearly seen in paintings on their pottery. The X-shaped frame gained in popularity, while a characteristically Greek chair, the *klismos*, has legs which curve inwards—a shape which has come to be known as 'sabre'. Turning on the lathe was a method used for shaping the legs of couches. Typical decorative motifs were the palmette, in a formalized shape; the 'key' pattern; and the human figure.

The Romans took over the Greek style, making it grander and with greater use of metal and stone. Massive tables were supported on slab ends sculpted from the solid rock. Others, made of bronze or silver, were elegantly conceived with an emphasis on vertical lines. Decorative devices included the anthemion (honeysuckle), trophies of arms, rams' heads and idealized representations of the human figure.

After the decline of the Roman Empire in the fifth century AD, many of the traditional crafts fell into disuse in what had been the Western Empire. In the Eastern capital of Byzantium (Constantinople — the modern Istanbul), the tradition of fine workmanship was maintained, with the classical styles of Greece and Rome intermixing with early Christian symbols and the abstract patterns favoured in the Middle East. Saints were depicted within borders of foliage and animals, which were elaborately carved on ivory boxes or painted on large wooden cupboards.

These cupboards form a connecting link between the Byzantine style and that known as Romanesque. (This is a confusing term, used to mean different things by different authorities. In the context of furniture, Romanesque is used to describe a style which, from the relatively few pieces extant, can be seen to have been established in the West in the thirteenth century, or possibly earlier, and which was current until the fourteenth century.) The typical Romanesque sacristy cupboard is painted inside and out with figures of saints in vivid colours and sometimes carved with 'arcading'—rounded arches supported on classical columns. Similar arcading is found on boxlike chests—a vestige of Roman architectural grandeur surviving into the Middle Ages, when political insecurity made the accumulation of much household furniture hardly worth while.

Gothic Gothic art, architecture and furniture has

little to do with the Goths, the German tribesmen who overran a large part of Europe following the collapse of the Roman Empire and reached the height of their power in Spain in the sixth century only to lose it again early in the eighth century. Gothic was originally a term of abuse hurled at the architecture of the Middle Ages by a pupil of Michelangelo whose object was to advance the interests of the 'new' style (now known as Renaissance) at the expense of the old. The style he wrongly termed Gothic actually began in twelfth-century France and flourished over much of Europe, especially the north, for the following four centuries. It is now used to describe a splendid, soaring style typified by the pointed arches and rose windows of cathedrals, and found repeated in miniature on much of the furniture that has survived. Like the buildings, this is solidly constructed and elaborately carved with foliage, and human and animal heads. Panels are often carved with what is called 'linenfold'—which was originally meant to represent scrolls of parchment. Typical pieces were chests of massive construction, often fitted with elaborate ironwork; high-backed armchairs with boxlike seats; tables mounted on trestles that could be taken apart easily, and stools which were made on rather the same pattern, with shaped slab ends. Much Gothic furniture was of oak and now strikes a rather gloomy note, but probably most of it was originally painted in carnival colours. The Gothic style enjoyed revivals in the eighteenth and nineteenth centuries.

Renaissance In 1453, when Byzantium fell to the Turks, the centre of Christendom returned to Rome. With it came some at least of the skills which had been preserved in the capital of the Eastern Empire. These made their contribution to the growing revival of interest in the classical culture of Greece and Rome, which had begun shortly after 1400 as a conscious movement, led by scholars, architects, artists and sculptors, but which was in reality a reawakening of the classical tradition that had lasted, in Italy, throughout the Romanesque and Gothic periods. Between 1500 and 1600, most European countries benefited from the resurgence, and many of them made their individual contributions to furniture design. In Italy, motherland of the Renaissance, rich decoration in carving and painting was lavished on the most important piece of furniture, the chest or *cassone*. France produced some splendidly carved walnut cupboards and cabinets in which the classical column and pilaster appear, the panels of the doors being decorated with carved 'strapwork' or formal inlaid designs. The chairs made during this period were high-backed with columnar legs. In Germany Gothic shapes were retained but decorated with carving in the Italian style, inspired by Greek and Roman mythology, a favourite subject being the nude figure surrounded by entwined foliage, and grotesque monsters. This decorative style developed into a recognizable type known as Mannerism. English Renaissance furniture also retained a Gothic flavour, but made much use of boldly turned legs on tables and bed posts. Carving was richer and more fluid than in the earlier, more austere Gothic.

In general, Renaissance furniture, though it sometimes included religious motifs in its carved or painted decoration, was increasingly secular and even pagan in spirit.

FAR LEFT
*French Renaissance
cabinet, second half of the
16th century, in the style
of the designer Ducerceau.
The use of architectural
columns and the carving
of a mythological figure
on the panel reflect the
revival of interest in the
culture of Greece and
Rome which inspired so
much Renaissance work.*
LEFT
*English oak chair, dated
1641, characteristic of
the late Renaissance style
in Britain at a time when
the Baroque was already
established in Southern
Europe.*
BELOW
*Italian prie-dieu
(prayer stool) decorated
in the transitional phase
between the Mannerist
style of the later
Renaissance, of which the
isolated nude figures are
typical, and the more
involved Baroque carving
of the early 17th century.*

ABOVE
*Eighteenth-century
Venetian Rococo settee,
carved and gilt, its
Italian flamboyance
slightly subdued by
French influence, making
it essentially a feminine
piece of furniture with a
lighthearted charm.*
RIGHT
*Baroque armchair in
walnut by Andrea
Brustolon of Venice, the
most outstanding sculptor
in 17th-century Italy to
turn his attention to
furniture. He handled the
bold, heavy style with
great confidence, but with
a delicate treatment of
the finer details.*

Baroque The Mannerist style of the late Renaissance was followed in seventeenth-century Italy and, ultimately, in most other European countries, by the much more involved Baroque style, which derived from the highly dramatic architecture and sculpture of the period. The human figure, for example, which had been neatly placed by the Mannerists at regular intervals, joined by bands of carved scrollwork, was now depicted in more lively postures, the limbs interwined with the foliage. The total effect in the more elaborate furniture is both monumental and restless, and indeed the greatest Italian makers, such as Andrea Brustolon, were famed as sculptors. Carving was executed in great depth. Hooklike scrolls gradually replaced the vertical line for legs, but where it was retained, the line was embellished with complex turning on the lathe. Baroque means 'irregular pearl', but most Baroque furniture is essentially symmetrical in design.

This is especially true of the French version,

strictly disciplined under such designers as Charles Le Brun and Jean Bérain, while Daniel Marot in the Netherlands, Paul Decker in Germany, Johannes Indau in Austria and William Kent in Britain were among those who influenced the work of designers in other countries. Some of these virtuoso performers worked simultaneously in two styles. Kent, for example, as late as the 1730's, was designing Italianate furniture with a strongly sculptural flavour for his coolly classical Palladian interiors. As well as these grand products, there was also Baroque furniture of a simpler kind, with features that again became international. These included the spiral or 'barley-sugar twist', the decoration of flat surfaces with applied mouldings and split turnery (see p.81) and the increased use of inlaid decoration, not only in the solid wood but also as marquetry (see p.6).

Rococo A reaction against the masculine pomp of the Baroque style began in France about 1715.

No style can ever be said to be entirely the brain child of one man, but it was the designing of Justin-Aurèle Meissonier—an artist of Italian origins—and the cabinetmaking of Charles Cressent that led the way towards a lighter, much more feminine style that employed amusing idioms—shells, rocks, *chinoiseries* with a romanticized flavour—and delicate, curving lines typified by the elongated S-shaped sweep of the cabriole leg. If the Baroque was melodrama, the Rococo was light comedy. At its height, it reached absurdity but managed to remain charming, with a marked tendency towards asymmetry in the carving of mirror frames and the backs of chairs, and in the fashioning of metal handles and mounts. Marquetry decoration was used for floral designs, painting to depict the delights of flirtation in rural surroundings. Rococo was essentially a style for the boudoir, but as interpreted by Thomas Chippendale in Britain, and his followers in America and some European countries, it was definitely more cautious than the French.

ABOVE
Italian carved and gilt throne chair, exhibiting to the full the high Baroque style with its love of elaboration and fantastic interplay of curves. The transition to a lighter style, however, is already heralded by the use of opposed C-shaped curves, which was to become a characteristic of the Rococo.

31

Neoclassical From about 1760 the curls and swirls of the Rococo were gradually replaced with a more severe line. Geometry was preferred to eccentricity, the straight leg to the cabriole, and where curves were permitted they were based on the circle, the oval and an uncomplicated version of the serpentine. This return to discipline was inspired partly by sheer boredom with the excesses of the Rococo, and partly by a wave of enthusiasm for the architecture and décor of Greece and Rome, which was given a great boost by excavations at Pompeii and Herculaneum. The attitude was at first romantic rather than pedantic, little attempt being made to reproduce the actual shapes of classical furniture, only their ornaments: urns, rams' heads, trophies of arms, painted scenes from Greek mythology.

This state of affairs lasted until about 1800, when a much more scholarly approach began to be taken by architects and designers such as Charles Percier and Pierre François Léonard Fontaine in France, Thomas Hope in Britain, Duncan Phyfe in America, Karl Friedrich Schinkel in Prussia and Leo von Klenze in Bavaria, who studied ancient furniture and produced designs in which the shapes as well as the ornaments are essentially faithful to the originals. To Roman and Greek forms they added Assyrian, Etruscan and Egyptian. This last contribution gained notably in popularity following Napoleon's Egyptian campaign. Indeed, Napoleon's influence was so strong that the period from about 1800 to 1820 is known generically as Empire, regardless of nationality. Its chief ingredients—the sabre-leg chair derived from the Greek *klismos*, the Greek-style couch, the circular table—lingered on

Neoclassical cabinet made by Jacob brothers, who worked in partnership until the death of the elder in 1803. They were commissioned to make most of the furniture for the residences of Napoleon. This cabinet, made by them during the period 1796–1803, has much more charm than is evident in much Empire furniture, but is still true to the academic spirit of the second phase of Neoclassicism.

as the Biedermeier style: severe in outline, solid, comfortable, middle-class.

Romantic revivals About 1830 the austere lines of the Biedermeier style were softened by a revival of the Rococo, especially of the cabriole leg. While some eighteenth-century designs were copied more or less accurately, there was also an unmistakably nineteenth-century style which, although it borrowed heavily from all past periods and mixed them up indiscriminately, nevertheless cannot be lightly dismissed. The general aim was usually to outdo the originals, so that proportions were exaggerated, lines distorted and decoration, especially carving, lavished with a curious lack of exuberance. This absence of spontaneity was inevitable when commercial manufacturers were putting together concoctions that included Baroque twists, Gothic arches and Rococo curves, all in the same piece of furniture, and using machinery for as much of the work as possible.

Honourable exceptions were the Gothic revivalist Augustus Welby Pugin and the medievalist William Burges in Britain; the executant of late Viennese Rococo, Carl Leistler; John Henry Belter of New York, whose Rococo intricacies triumphed by their sheer self-confidence; the Danish exponent of Neoclassicism, Gustav Hetsch; Eugène Emmanuel Viollet-le-Duc in France, an architect and designer with a genuine knowledge of past styles; and in Italy, the creators of the style called Dantesque, who sought inspiration from the Renaissance for furniture, especially chairs, of fine quality, carved in walnut. Even the best of these designers, however, were nostalgic rather than forward-looking.

English dining chair in mahogany, of the Regency period, c. 1815, with sabre-shaped leg based on the ancient Greek klismos. Georges Jacob was one of the first to employ this shape for chair legs, in late 18th-century France. It became generally popular throughout Europe and Ameria during the first quarter of the 19th century.

Lady's chair of the early Victorian period, c. 1845, in the style then quaintly described as 'Elizabethan', but in fact combining such elements of the Baroque as the barleysugar twist with the cabriole leg of the Rococo.

The Arts and Crafts Movement In the mid-nineteenth century principles of design and craftsmanship were expressed in the writings of John Ruskin and the Comte Léon de Laborde, who put most of the blame for the degeneration of taste on mechanization. An attempt to put their theories into practice was made in England in the 1860's by William Morris, whose workshops produced furniture of varying quality, hand-made and often fitted with hand-wrought metalwork. Morris was associated with the Pre-Rephaelite school of painters, and some of the finest furniture from his workshops, such as that designed by Philip Webb, is decorated with painted panels. Here was a conscientious attempt at creativity, but a love of medieval ornament and a failure to make proper use of modern industrial methods imposed strict limitations both on Morris and his followers.

Art Nouveau Adventurousness in design did not really escape from its moorings until the Paris Exhibition of 1889, when the style best known as Art Nouveau was successfully launched. It had about a dozen different names in as many countries, Art Nouveau being that of a shop in Paris, owned by a German named S. Bing, who had originally been an importer of oriental works of art. Japanese art was one of the powerful influences on artists and designers of this new style, who included men of many nationalities, each contributing something characteristic of his native country. The movement had been growing in strength since about 1870, its more austere elements coming from C. F. A. Voysey, Charles Rennie Mackintosh and Arthur H. Mackmurdo in Britain, who designed pieces which were usually (but not always) angular and often devoid of ornament. Mackmurdo, especially, sometimes used the sinuous, plantlike forms more

often associated with the French practitioners, Louis Majorelle and Emile Gallé of Nancy; the Belgian, Henri van de Velde; and the American, Louis Tiffany. In Norway Gerhard Munthe created the 'Viking' style, using peasant traditions in which bird motifs appear as proudly as on the prows of Viking ships. In Germany, August Endell of Munich was one of those greatly influenced by Chinese and Japanese forms, while C. A. Lion Cachet of Holland introduced Javanese motifs. A group of Viennese designers—Otto Wagner, Josef Hoffmann, Josef Olbrich and Adolf Loos—reacted against the more extravagant use of Neorococo curves and excessive ornament, and pursued a policy of producing functional furniture at low cost. Workshops dedicated to this principle were founded in Vienna in 1903.

Art Deco The furniture of the jazz age is characterized by what were known in the 1920's as 'futurist' designs: bold, curving cabinet work made possible by the use of plywood; brightly contrasted upholstery fabrics; sheer surfaces relieved by chromium-plated mounts and handles. The most distinguished designer in this area was Jacques-Emile Ruhlmann, a spectacular Parisian who expanded a family house-painting business into a highly fashionable establishment for the creation of custom-built furniture, using the finest veneers in conjunction with metal and ivory fittings. By 1925 he was able to command prices in excess of those being obtained at the time for the work of the most distinguished eighteenth-century French cabinet-makers, such as Georges Jacob, some of whose designs no doubt served to inspire Ruhlmann. But Ruhlmann was no copyist. He had an original talent combined with a respect for the past, and stamped his own name on his work in the tradition of the eighteenth-century masters.

The Modernists

On a rather different track during the early years of the twentieth century were the inheritors of the Arts and Crafts Movement in Britain—Sidney Barnsley and Ernest Gimson, who produced good furniture by hand, mostly to special order, and Ambrose Heal, who designed in a dignified but more commercial way for his London store. The American architect Frank Lloyd Wright began experimenting in 1904 with stark constructions composed of boards mounted on frames. During World War I, a Dutch joiner named Gerrit Rietveld evolved ideas for abstract design in furniture, which were set forth in the influential magazine *de Stijl*, a name which has since been applied to the group to which Rietveld belonged. Many of their ideas were acted on after the war when Walter Gropius set up at Dassau in Germany a school of art and architecture, known as the Bauhaus. Here an appreciation of the lightness and simplicity of Japanese furniture was related to the needs of modern methods of production. One of the leading Bauhaus designers was Marcel Breuer, a Hungarian who pioneered the use of tubular metal frames. Experiments in this material had already been carried out successfully by Mart Stam and Mies van der Rohe of Holland. Though these experimental pieces were hand-made, they led to the mass production of tubular and strip metal furniture.

The Swiss architect Charles-Edouard Jeanneret—better known as Le Corbusier—helped to found a magazine, *L'Esprit Nouveau*, and in 1923 published a book, *Vers une Architecture*. He declared, 'We do not believe in decorative art,' and in 1925 defined domestic 'equipment' as 'cases, seats and tables'. He began designing functional furniture in the following year, partly under the influence of Michael Thonet, a nineteenth-century Austrian famous for his bentwood furniture, and also of Stam and Breuer.

In Denmark Kaare Klint was influenced by Le Corbusier but also studied classical design and eighteenth-century English and American models. His apparently unadventurous style was of major importance in creating the contemporary Scandinavian school of design.

Alvar Aalto, born in Finland in 1899, first experimented with furniture in tubular metal and then turned to the beechwood forests of his native land for a material—laminated plywood—which could be bent and moulded to produce shapes in wood that would normally have been possible only in metal. All his designs are eminently suited to mass production without any reduction in the quality of the product.

Charles Eames, born in 1907, has been described as 'the first American furniture designer of international significance'. He was trained under the Finnish-born architect Eliel Saarinen, with whose son Eero he shared a prize for organic design in home furnishings in 1940. Since then Eames has continued to design furniture that combines elegance with practicality, and his work has been a major influence both in America and Europe.

It cannot be denied that this century has, under commercial pressure and popular demand, produced some of the shoddiest and ugliest furniture ever made in the history of civilization; but a growing awareness both of good design and the use of modern methods and man-made materials points the way towards a furnishing style of great purity and simplicity.

THE BED

OPPOSITE
Tyrolean bed in painted wood. As in the example of the African footrest, the importance of the marriage bed is emphasized by this example of a bridal bed inscribed with the bride's name and the date of the wedding, 1771.

BELOW
Most societies place more emphasis on the headboard than on the footboard of a bed. This footboard is used by the Yombe group of tribes in the Western Congo during the initiation of puberty rites for unmarried girls in the 'fattening house'. The figures depict a girl with her bridegroom and an old man, her uncle, who is unhappy because he has negotiated the marriage on terms which please neither family.

Even among the least sophisticated peoples, there is always somewhere to lay one's head. The type of headrest still in use in New Guinea comes in a variety of shapes and sizes, but is usually carved with human heads, which often have an extra pair of eyes—to guard, so anthropologists conclude, against evil spirits who might enter the sleeper's head, were he to lay it on the ground. Sometimes there are less fanciful reasons for the headrest. In Fiji the islanders are proud of their elaborate hair styles, so there the headrest supports the base of the skull, leaving the *coiffure* undisturbed—a matter of some importance, as both hair style and headrest are regarded as status symbols. The bed of the New Zealand Maori is a mat of wood bark, which is only eclipsed in social importance by his cloak.

The Egyptians had bedsteads during the Middle Kingdom (1575–1075 BC), with footboards that were often decorated with carving, gilding and inlay. There was no board at the head of the bed, but a headrest was placed between the two posts, providing a convenient link between the beds of primitive and advanced societies. The ancient Greek bed, which was used as a couch by day, had no footboard, but employed a fixed rest for the head. The frame was of wood, sometimes veneered with ivory, standing on carved or turned legs. A form of springing was provided by a platform made out of strips of leather, and on this support animal skins were spread. By about 200 BC, Greek and Roman couches were being made of bronze and fitted with both headrests and footrests, shaped like swans' necks. Towards the

end of the first century AD, simplified versions of the Roman bed or couch were in use as far north as the Rhineland, but more usually the Teutonic tribes slept on animal skins spread on the floor, or at best in a kind of shallow, wooden chest.

Things had improved in Northern Europe by the thirteenth century. Framed bedsteads of wood, with carved and painted decoration, were used as couches in the daytime and curtained off at night. The importance of these hangings increased in the later Middle Ages, when the rich owner, whenever he went on a long journey, would have them carried around the country with him for his nightly use, the crude wooden frames remaining in position ready to receive them. The hangings comprised, as well as curtains that could be drawn, an overhead canopy or tester, and the 'celure', which hung above the pillows before the introduction of the wooden headboard, and was frequently embroidered with the owner's coat of arms, proclaiming pride in his family. After about 1500, this badge was often carved on the wooden headboard, which was at first placed—like the ancient Egyptian headrest—between two posts. These, together with another pair at the foot, supported the tester and gave rise to the term 'four-poster'. The name persisted after 1550, although by that time the headboard had become substantial enough to support its end of the tester, and the posts at the head of the bed were often dispensed with, leaving only those at the foot, which were, in Renaissance times, boldly turned and richly carved.

One reason for the long persistence of this type of bed was that, by drawing the curtains together, a measure of privacy could be ensured. In most countries, the idea of a bedroom as such was unknown until the eighteenth century. Until then the room in which the bed stood was, as often as not, a living room by day, in the homes of princes and peasants alike. In late sixteenth-century Holland, Germany and Sweden, magnificently carved bedsteads were built into such rooms as integral parts of the architecture, with panelling to match, while in Brittany, Scotland and Wales, the living rooms of farmhouses continued to have cupboard beds, enclosed by doors, until well into the nineteenth century. Even after rooms were set aside to serve specifically as sleeping quarters, perfectly healthy people in polite society received guests while lying in bed, and in many parts of Europe and America the full-tester bedstead, complete with drapes, survived long after the original idea of a room within a room had ceased to be a necessity. The bedstead reflected changes of fashion in the choice of wood and the turning of the posts, which became slimmer and more elegant as the eighteenth century advanced, and by incorporating such modish features as the cabriole leg with lion's paw foot popular in the 1740's, or the alternative Marlboro' leg, straight and square, which was a feature of Philadelphia beds about 1770.

A half-tester or 'angel' bed was a novelty introduced in France as early as 1672. It had no posts at all but a canopy projecting from the wall above the head of the bed. About 1750, in Portugal, the bed lost its tester completely and a revolutionary type appeared, with a handsome, dome-shaped headboard and a foot that not only had cabriole feet coming to the floor, but a continuation of them in reverse, as it were, projecting into the air. This type is still popular with manufacturers of reproduction furniture, who call it 'Queen Anne'. At about the same time, a bed with a low headboard, often with painted decoration, appeared in Spain. The Russians were producing, about 1750, an adult-sized crib on cabriole legs, with shaped boards at head and foot and armrests at both ends—rather as though two settees had been placed facing each other and joined with a mattress in the middle. A German innovation was a feather-filled quilt to provide warmth without excessive weight. The French, towards the middle of the eighteenth

century, scrapped the bedposts and introduced a bed with elaborate headboard and footboard, set sideways into a draped alcove—a style that continued, with suitable decorative amendments, into the Empire period. The Danes adopted the same method of placing the bed in an alcove, using checked linen drapes in place of damask.

These, of course, were the beds of the well-to-do. The bed of the poor man was often no more than a straw-filled mattress on the floor, or sometimes simply the floor itself. Personal servants in the houses of rich men thought it a privilege to sleep on a truckle bed—a low frame mounted on wheels, which was pushed underneath the master's high four-poster during the day—and in some houses, remained there at night as well with the servant asleep on it. Between these extremes of rich and poor there existed peasant communities for whom the norm was a wooden bedstead with a simple, panelled headboard and low, turned posts at the foot. In Alpine countries these were often painted in gay colours, while in Scandinavia they were built of pine, sometimes relieved with shallow, carved decoration.

ABOVE
English brass bedstead decorated with mother-of-pearl, late 19th century, with a Victorian patchwork quilt. Although it came to be despised as oldfashioned by sophisticated people in Western Europe and North America during the first half of the 20th century, the brass bedstead continued to be made and returned to fashion in the 1960's.

The French always attached enormous importance to the bed as a status symbol, the king's bed being held in higher regard even than the throne itself, and all who could afford to do so lavished great trouble and expense in emulating this grandeur. Yet it was the French who, in the second half of the eighteenth century, first introduced the simple iron bedstead—the forerunner of the bed found today in many hospitals and institutions. Brass bedsteads were first made in Birmingham, England, about 1830, and have continued in production for more than a century in varying qualities—some of solid brass tubing, some of brass-plated iron, some decorated with mother-of-pearl. These symbols of Victorian respectability were still being made for export into the 1950's—not as reproductions of the antique but as straightforward, 'contemporary' products—to South America, Egypt and Turkey.

Wooden bedsteads, however, had never ceased to be made, and some remarkable constructions in mahogany, walnut and olive, with massively turned members, made in the nineteenth and early twentieth centuries, still remain immovable in many parts of Europe—especially the country districts of France, Italy and Greece. Less monumental specimens, with slatted ends and bits of inlaid decoration mildly suggestive of Art Nouveau, came into fashion about 1900, to be replaced in popularity 20 years later by beds with low, solid-looking boards at head and foot with sheer, veneered surfaces. These had wire mesh mattresses resting on side-irons, with overlays stuffed with horsehair or wool. An alternative was the box mattress, in which coil springs were completely enclosed by a striped cotton covering known as 'ticking'. This has since been replaced with the interior-sprung mattress—an extension of the same principle—and more recently by the mattress made out of foam rubber. With these changes came the popularization of the modern divan bed in the 1930's, with its own feet resting on the floor, thus eliminating the need for cast iron supports for the mattress, and for a footboard to attach them to the headboard.

The contemporary headboard is often as wooden and hard and comfortless as a Fijian headrest; far more sympathetic to weary shoulder blades is the quilted headboard. But comfort apart, any modern bed that attempts to be more than purely functional is still, like the grand beds of the past, a kind of talisman, helping to ward off any evil spirit that threatens the owner's sense of security. The bed may adopt an unusual shape—circular beds hold a glamour for some—or simply be exceptionally large. It may be a water-bed, with the latest fashion in water-filled, electrically heated mattresses—although the first advertisement for a water-filled mattress appeared in the London *Times* in 1854. It may have a headboard equipped with reading lamps, telephones, hi-fi. It may be adjustable to various angles. One reaction to this kind of thing is the growing practice among many young people of making do with a mattress on the floor—a trend, perhaps, towards the unaffected traditions of their primitive ancestors, which represents also a refusal to worry too much about financial security. It is significant that in many countries the laws affecting bankruptcy still allow a debtor to retain his bed when everything else is seized. Even today, in some peasant communities—the Greek islands, for example—money is therefore lavished on the bed, although the rest of the home may be frugally furnished.

ABOVE
Richly painted bedstead, English, second half of the 19th century, designed by the architect William Burges, who revived the medieval style in an imaginative way, working mainly for rich patrons such as the Marquess of Bute. During the same period, many less expensive but more monumental bedsteads were made.

RIGHT
In the 1970's the four-poster bed, like the brass bedstead, enjoyed a return to favour. This simple construction in pine produced commercially by an English manufacturer has drapes at head and foot but no headboard. It resembles the medieval four-poster of plain wood, acting as a framework for drapes.

THE SEAT

Any kind of seat made to isolate the occupant from his immediate surroundings and fellow creatures, whether it takes the form of a mat or rug, stool, chair or sofa, can be traced to the idea of a throne—a seat of honour; and to this day, the most important man or woman present at a meeting is asked to be 'chairman' or to 'take the chair'.

In many African villages, the only piece of furniture is the chief's stool, accepted by the tribesmen as the seat of power and invested with magical properties. The dating of such primitive furniture presents problems, and there are few African stools that can be placed with certainty much earlier than the nineteenth century. Most of the traditional forms have probably changed little in hundreds of years, but European influence is to be detected in some, especially those with very low seats. Some European chairs evolved in the same way, by adding backs to stools, and are known as 'back-stools'. Many African ceremonial stools are elaborately carved, and in one East African example, dating from about 1900, a man on a bicycle was included among the traditional themes. These vary greatly from area to area. Human figures are portrayed by the Bini in Nigeria, while abstract designs are preferred by the Angruman tribe in Ghana. In Western Nigeria, the Yoruba used quartz to fashion a simple, cylindrical column with a snake-like attachment like a handle projecting from one side. Whether the style is severe or ornate, the sense of dignity and power is always present in these stools.

The typical well-to-do Egyptian in Tutankh-amun's reign would have owned about half-a-dozen stools, varying in type from a popular four-legged construction with underframing in painted wood to more elaborate forms of inlaid ebony on X-shaped supports made to fold flat. But such a home would also boast a chair—only one—with or without arms, the legs carved to simulate those of a lion, the back panelled, the flat seat made of woven cord. The stools had 'dished' seats, much more sympathetic to the human posterior; but it was the chair, in some ways less comfortable, that was occupied by the head of the house.

In ancient Greece and Rome the X-shaped stool, in both folding and rigid forms, appears in paintings as the seat for a deity or man of authority. In Rome it became the *curule*—the magistrate's stool; but it was the chair in wood or bronze with inward-curving legs that came to be favoured more and more as a throne. After the fall of Rome the X-framed chair became the more usual type in Byzantium.

In the Gothic period the stool gradually became a workaday article made of solid wood, with slab ends splaying outwards and joined below by a stretcher that passed through slots cut in them, secured by wedges. The seat was often a hinged lid over a boxlike compartment, relating the stool to the chest. By the end of the sixteenth century this construction was superseded by the 'joyned' stool with four turned legs joined to the seat frame and the understretchers by the mortise and tenon joint: the end of the rail is fined down to a tongue which fits into a cavity cut into the square section of the leg and is secured by dowel pins driven through it. Dowel pins also fixed the seat to the frame.

The early Gothic chair of the second half of the fifteenth century very often has a box seat and may be seen in this instance to have evolved from the chest. The arms were enclosed by slabs of wood pegged or nailed to the framework in the earlier examples, and in later ones by panels contained within the framework. The back could be stiff and square or might rise to a pointed arch. Details of decoration, and even of shape, varied from country to country. In Portugal the shape was usually rectilinear but the carving very ornate. In Spain the construction was lighter, with a complex, triple-arched back and delicate carving. The French produced a tub-shaped armchair, while the English Gothic chair tended to be boxlike, with linenfold panelling, except in a few very special examples intended for use by royalty and princes of the church. Ecclesiastical architecture has a very strong influence on most of the furniture that has survived from this period—partly because church furniture has been better protected from the ravages of everyday use, and partly because the feudal lords used such furniture as models. In Northern Europe chairs remained few in number until the middle of the sixteenth century, their use in even the grandest castles being restricted to the lord, his lady and one or two high-ranking guests. Everyone else sat on stools or on benches, which were simply elongated stools.

In Renaissance Italy, about 1500, simple chairs began to be made in quantity. They had no arms, and were really back-stools, with slat ('ladder') backs and rushed seats. They soon came to be regarded as humble objects; for wealthy people quite grand chairs were made with high backs and

OPPOSITE
Chair on X-shaped supports, Florentine, c. 1550. Known as 'Savonarola' or 'Luther' the type is descended from the Roman curule, and variations occur in many countries over a very long period. It was sometimes made to fold flat.

RIGHT
African stool, carved wood, from the Congo. The ceremonial seat of a local king of the Ngombe tribe, its primary function is that of a throne, but such stools were often used, when occasion demanded, as tables. This is true of many stools the world over, and some which are now antiques are used today as coffee tables.

padded seats, which were variously mounted on X-shaped supports, turned columns or square legs relieved with fluting. This style soon spread to France, where an important concession to women was made in the form of the *caquetoire* or 'gossip' chair, with a wide seat that allowed room for fashionably full skirts. Another blow for female emancipation was struck about 1600 in the Netherlands, with the introduction of the 'farthingale' chair, as it became known in England, where it was made at about the same time. (The farthingale was the hooped metal frame over which the skirt was extended, and its width made it difficult for women to sit in a chair with arms.) Again, this chair was really a stool with a back added, framed up with understretchers joining legs which were sometimes square with chamfered corners, or turned on the lathe as simple columns. The seat and back were padded, and the wood used was usually

oak, although occasionally solid walnut was chosen.

Armchairs of the late sixteenth and early seventeenth centuries, on the other hand, were seldom padded, and were designed to minister to the user's sense of importance rather than his comfort. Both the panel in the back and the cresting rail above were usually carved, while the arms had a downward slope towards the front, and the legs were turned to resemble columns or bobbins. There was a craze for turning, expressed in an extreme form by one type of chair, known as a 'turned' chair, which continued to be made over a very long period and the origins of which are something of a mystery. One theory—hotly contested in some quarters—is that it was a type which went northwards from Byzantium to Scandinavia, and thence to Britain. It has a triangular seat, three turned legs and an assembly of turnings forming the back and arms.

French throne-chair, late 15th century. The panelled, boxlike seat relates it to the chest. The construction and the proportions are Gothic in style, but the open arms with turnings, the pediment carved with a shell and flanked by classical urns all point to the influence of the Italian Renaissance.

46

ABOVE LEFT
English Renaissance armchair, the shape showing French influence, the panels carved with Romayne work portrait medallions, mid 16th century.

ABOVE RIGHT
Late 16th-century caquetoire *or gossip chair. French in origin, this type of chair became popular in the Netherlands and, to a lesser extent, in Britain. The exceptional width between the arms made it a boon to women wearing the fashionably wide skirts of the period.*

The X-shaped frame made a fresh appearance in many countries about 1550, with the woodwork sometimes covered entirely in leather, in the Spanish style, or in velvet or even in embroidered satin. The great advantage of this shape for a chair was that it could be made to fold flat. Popularly associated with the Reformation, it is commonly known in Germany as a 'Luther' chair and in Italy as a 'Savonarola'. In Italy a period of social change in the early seventeenth century brought a powerful newly rich class into being, which demanded a greater degree of comfort and a more exuberant type of furniture, intended as much for display as for use. The velvets of Genoa and the silks of Lucca made such luxury readily available, and lent themselves well to the opulence of the Baroque style. Many Italian Baroque chairs are masterpieces of woodcarving, with legs formed like human figures, in the round, supporting elaborately scrolled arms. Grotesque masks, entwined foliage and romping *putti* (cherubs) are used to form underframings and cresting rails. Chairs in a much more restrained style, however, with turned legs and stretchers, scrolled arms, and upholstered seats and backs were to be found in the same houses, intended for family use. Germany adopted an eccentric side-effect of the Baroque style, to be seen in chairs with straight legs that curve out abruptly at the feet, as though bending under the strain, and high backs surmounted by carving in the 'auricular' style—the name given to a taste for treating the bones and membranes of the body in a style that resembled the curves and crevices of the human ear. This curious repertoire of ornament was first exploited early in the seventeenth century by Paul van Vianen, a Dutch silversmith who had studied anatomy in Prague. A more naive version

of it occurs in a type of chair that is characteristically Swiss, with a plain wooden seat on simple, splayed legs, all the grotesque decoration being concentrated on the carving of the low back.

The origins of North American furniture can be traced to events of the early seventeenth century. William Brewster was one of those who sailed on the *Mayflower* in 1620; he became the elder and teacher at Plymouth, Massachusetts, where John Carver was governor of the colony. Two traditional types of American chair are named after these Pilgrim Fathers. Both are simple, rustic chairs with solid seats and 'stick' backs composed of turned spindles. The 'Brewster' has additional spindles under the arms and under the seat, down to the front stretcher; or, according to some authorities, while the 'Carver' has only one row of spindles in the back, the 'Brewster' has two. The woods commonly used were maple, ash and hickory. American stick-back chairs owe something to Dutch, as well as English, prototypes—for example, the mushroom-shaped knop at the top of the arm support. This influence may partly be due to the fact that a number of the Pilgrims, including Brewster himself, lived for a time in Leyden before sailing for New England.

The Baroque style was rather slow to make an impact on English furniture. In its more domestic mood, exemplified by the square-backed chair on turned legs, it had begun to replace Renaissance furniture during the first half of the seventeenth century, but the coming of the Civil War followed by the Protectorate of Oliver Cromwell delayed progress. The Cromwellian chair is square and rather provincial-looking, constructed of oak with leather on back and seat, but not always as severe in conception as modern notions of Puritan England might suggest. The leather was sometimes tooled

BELOW
*English oak armchair,
early to mid 17th
century, the panelled
back with carved
decoration.
Characteristically, it
does more for the user's
dignity than for his
comfort.*

RIGHT
*Early American
stickback chair of the
type known as
Brewster, New England,
c. 1650–1690. Made of
ash, maple and pine, it is
named after one of the
Pilgrim Fathers.*
BELOW RIGHT
*Swiss chair in the
auricular style, also
popular in Germany in
the 17th century, which
exploits grotesque
elements of the Baroque.*

49

and coloured in the Spanish style, and this type of square armchair is, in fact, strongly reminiscent of the Spanish 'monk's chair' of the late sixteenth and early seventeenth centuries. This Spanish influence probably reached Britain from the Netherlands, which had only recently escaped from Spanish rule and where crafts such as the tooling of leather had long been practized with great success.

Spain produced some extravagantly ornate Baroque chairs—probably inspired by Florentine and Venetian models—which were a mass of convoluted curves, originally painted in bright colours or gilded. Again, they were mainly status symbols, and in more general use alongside them were much more sober specimens, rectilinear in shape and with turned frames. Portuguese chairs emphasized this turning, the ball feet especially being very pronounced, but with a boldness balanced by backs which were arched at the top and dipped to a shaped apron below.

France imported the Baroque style from Italy early in the seventeenth century and developed it during the Louis XIII period. The style remained strongly Italianate, with great emphasis on florid carving, until Louis XIV came of age and began his personal rule in 1661. Even discounting the royal silver throne itself, chairs were quite splendid, and they gradually became more comfortable, with lower seats, the backs raked at an angle, the arms curving downwards so that human arms could rest on them more easily.

Legs, which on most chairs had been spiral or

bobbin-turned during the reign of Louis XIII, now developed a scroll shape; if turning was employed, it was to produce a well-defined protuberance, like an inverted cup, near the top of the leg, and a tapered shaft below it. A similar profile was also achieved in square section, without turning. This style of leg became immensely popular in Holland, and is often mistakenly thought of as being Dutch in origin.

King Charles II of England lived in Holland for most of the decade before his restoration to the throne in 1660. The Dutch, by now a powerful maritime nation, were busily building Amsterdam and furnishing its tall, narrow houses with handsome furniture. Charles easily acquired the taste for such luxury and when he returned to England, the high Baroque style went with him. His wife, Catherine of Braganza, added a Portuguese flavour to the taste of the English court for a while, although it was Charles's flamboyant love of extravance that dominated the styles until William and Mary's reign.

Now, by a curious irony, English furniture design began to influence that of other European countries. The highly destructive Great Fire of London in 1666 made the replacement of large quantities of furniture an urgent necessity, and extra timber had to be imported from Norway, which was then politically tied to Denmark. Faced with the problem of paying for the timber, the English re-exported some of it, now made up into furniture, to Denmark, where the chairs in particular were so well liked that the pattern went on being reproduced there long after it had gone out of fashion in Britain.

RIGHT
English oak chair, country-made, c. 1675, with panelled back. A drawer for pipes and tobacco is fitted under the seat. In pious homes, the drawer was used to hold a Bible.

BELOW LEFT
English 'sleeping' chair c. 1675, the gilded frame composed of spirals joined by carved stretchers, the winged, adjustable back making this an article of comfort as well as grandeur.

BELOW RIGHT
Late 17th-century chair-back carved in the style associated with the designs of Daniel Marot, cabinetmaker to William of Orange. Walnut was used for the best examples, but oak and beech were often employed.

The typical Charles II chair (otherwise known as 'Restoration') was, in the first place, largely Franco-Dutch in style. It was made either of walnut—the fashionable wood of the period—of beech stained to look like walnut, or of oak. The seats and the high, narrow backs with their arched cresting rails were usually caned. The weaving of split cane was a technique that had been brought from the Orient by the East India trading companies. The 'barley-sugar twist' was very popular. Originally, it was carved by hand but it soon came within the capacity of the turner. Normally, English twists are cut deeper than Dutch, but the English craftsmen sometimes deliberately imitated the shallower spiral of the Netherlands. About 1680 the scroll-shaped leg, already popular in Italy and France, was introduced; but whether turned or scrolled, the front legs of chairs usually had a flat, shaped stretcher between them, carved to match the cresting rail with a crown flanked by two cherubs—a device said to mark the restora-

tion of the monarchy but in fact already popular in Holland before Charles II was crowned.

Many chairs were richly upholstered, in spite of the high cost of imported textiles, and some were fitted with 'wings'. Framed settees were conceived as three chairs of the high-backed type joined together. Daybeds had caned platforms resting on six or eight legs, with a back, sometimes adjustable, at one end. Adjustable arms were also a feature of fully upholstered settees of the type now known as 'Knole', after the great house of that name where some have been preserved. Very few genuine specimens of these have survived, however.

Charles's niece Mary and her husband William of Orange ascended the English throne in 1689, thereby linking Britain and Holland. It was a time when both countries were absorbing a large number of Huguenot refugees from France, many of whom were highly skilled craftsmen. One of these was Daniel Marot, who entered the service of William of Orange as a cabinetmaker. Many of

Dutch armchair, c. 1600–1625, with velvet upholstery on a rosewood frame. Upholstered chairs were an expensive luxury at this time, especially in Northern Europe.

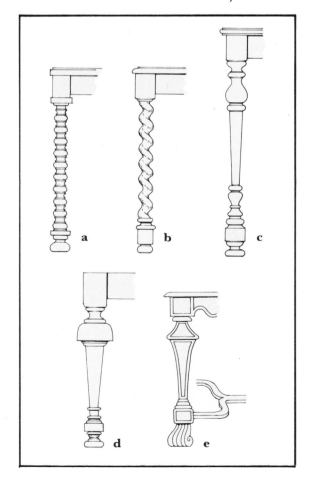

Turned legs in general use for chairs and other furniture of Anglo-Dutch type, 1640–1700:
a. *1640–1660;*
b. *1660–1680;*
c. *1685–1700;*
d. *1685–1700;*
e. *1680–1700.*

Marot's designs were published and a particular type of chair, with a leg of the inverted-cup type and a high arched back, which was elaborately fretted and carved, is permanently associated with his name.

The William-and-Mary style in both Britain and America, though basically Dutch, soon acquired national and even regional characteristics. This is seen in the turning of legs—the Dutch leg inclining to heaviness, the English being substantial but trim, and the American delicate, sometimes to the point of structural weakness. Even so, the American version of the style, which lasted well into the eighteenth century, is the most gracious. The scroll leg occurs on very few pieces of American furniture, and even in England it was adopted with some caution. By about 1700 it was being smoothed into the elegant curve of the cabriole leg, which developed fully in the early years of Queen Anne's reign (1702–14), and was to dominate so much furniture for the next half-century.

RIGHT
English armchair employing split canework, and carved with the 'boyes and crowne' device characteristic of the Charles II period, but also popular in Holland and Scandinavia.
BELOW
Development of the scroll leg into the cabriole curve for chairs and other furniture of Anglo-Dutch type, 1660–1760:
a. *1670–1685;*
b. *1680–1690;*
c. *1690–1700;*
d. *1700–1760;*
e. *1715–1760.*

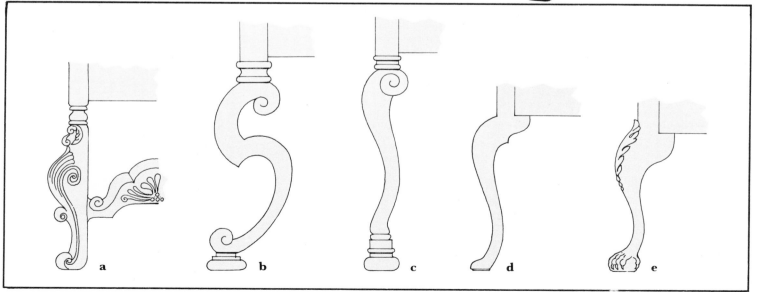

a   b   c   d   e

The 'Queen Anne' style, as it is known in Britain and America, was also popular in a number of countries where English influence was strong. The characteristic chair of the period has a back composed of graceful curves, like the necks of swans meeting, around a central, vase-shaped splat. The seat may be angular, wider at the front than at the back, but is often rounded, the front rail varying in shape according to local preferences. The legs are cabriole, and in early versions are united near the feet with turned stretchers. These stretchers were soon discarded in England and in New York, but in Philadelphia, for example, they were retained until about the middle of the eighteenth century. In Boston many chairs were decorated in imitation of oriental lacquer.

Arms were shaped into generous curves to correspond with those of the legs, which could terminate in any one of a variety of forms—the simple 'pad' foot on early examples, the lion's paw, hoof and ball and claw occurring after 1715. The shell, symbol of the Rococo style, is often found carved on the knee of the chair leg and again on the cresting rail at the top of the back. The wood used in England and Holland in the first quarter of the eighteenth century is usually walnut, but as mahogany became more fashionable, similar chairs are found in this material, but with fretted splats.

Portugal was one of the countries where English influence was particularly strong at this time. The widowed Catherine of Braganza returned to her native country in 1693, taking a great deal of English furniture with her. The Treaty of Methuen in 1703 resulted in a flourishing trade between the two countries. During the reign of John V (1706–50) English furniture was imported and copied, often in the hard jacaranda wood that came from the

ABOVE
One of a pair of English walnut chairs, early 18th century, with vase-shaped splats in the backs, standing on fully developed cabriole legs carved on the knees and terminating in claw feet.

RIGHT
Italian chair, mid 18th century, with japanned decoration in imitation of oriental lacquer. Some English influence is evident in the shaping of the back and legs, but their termination without well-defined feet is more French in feeling.

Portuguese colony of Brazil. Local variations were made in Brazil itself.

The English and Dutch furniture made during the first few decades of the eighteenth century have much in common, and the chairs of the two countries are hard to tell apart. The chief differences are a tendency for the Dutch cabriole leg to be heavier than the English, and for the front seat rails to be shaped in a more complex way. The splats of Dutch chairs are often decorated with marquetry. Seat furniture of an Anglo-Dutch type was also found at this time in Northern Germany and in Scandinavia, where the Dutch heaviness became even more marked in Swedish and Norwegian examples. The Danes, who prohibited the importation of foreign furniture for about 20 years in the middle of the century, and so cut themselves off from changes in fashion abroad, were still making chairs in the English 'Queen Anne' style in the 1760's. The Anglo-Dutch style was preferred by the European middle classes as well as the prosperous burghers of America, while the royal houses and the nobility of Europe generally preferred to model their furniture on the grander styles current in France, adopting a more exuberant version of the Rococo style.

Italy retained the heavy Baroque style in formal reception rooms, but adopted the Rococo for those that were devoted to easy-going family life. By the middle of the century, the Italians were making more use of it even in their public rooms, and in Venice especially some very elaborate sofas, long enough to seat half-a-dozen people, were made for ballrooms. Chairs were modelled closely on French originals, the Piedmontese being particularly successful with their copies, although the curves are rather exaggerated.

RIGHT
Portuguese chair, early 18th century, in jacaranda wood. English influence, fairly strong in Portugal during this period, is displayed in the general outline of back and legs, but the design remains Southern European in its exaggeration of curves.
BELOW
Italian settee, mid 18th century, of the exceptionally long type used in ballrooms, especially in Venice, where the heavy Baroque style favoured for public rooms was gradually ousted in favour of a lighter manner, influenced by the feminine flavour of French Rococo.

In Spain and her South American colonies enthusiasm for the style led to the exaggerated use of opposing C-shaped scrolls to produce asymmetrical effects, such as chairs with carved shells crowning their backs at a slightly drunken angle, like paper hats on inebriated party guests.

The Rococo style had begun its lively course in France about 1715, during the *Régence* of Philippe d'Orléans, and reached perfection during the reign of Louis XV (1723–74); although it died somewhat before he did it is permanently associated with his name. One of the style's most practical contributions lay in a whole range of elegant but comfortable seat furniture. The *fauteuil* had open arms with padded back and seat, while the writer Voltaire gave his name to a type with a very deep seat and sloping back. He noted that 'ladies can be seen reclining on sofas and daybeds without causing embarrassment to their friends'. The name *canapé* was a general one applied to a wide variety of such sofas, but the French have a whole vocabulary to distinguish between slightly different types. The French *bergère* is an armchair with padded back, enclosed arms and cushioned seat—not to be confused with the English use of the term, which implies a caned back and arms. All these French chairs and sofas were richly upholstered, often with tapestries specially designed so that the pattern fitted the shape of the frame, and those in the Louis XV style had cabriole legs of a particularly elegant form, many terminating in upward-scrolling feet. The exposed woodwork—walnut, oak or beech—was sometimes gilded, sometimes painted, sometimes left its natural colour and waxed. The legs are joined to the seat rails with mortise and tenon joints, secured by dowel pins, the ends of which can be seen on chairs left in the natural state. Veneering on the legs of French chairs is usually an indication of the fact that they were not manufac-

tured until the nineteenth century.

In the eighteenth century, the work was divided between guilds of craftsmen. This was a system which obtained to a greater or lesser extent in other countries but was especially highly organized in France, where despite raging jealousies between various guilds, a very high level of craftsmanship was maintained. From 1751 until the Revolution ended the practice in 1791, French craftsmen were normally required to stamp their work with their names, unless excused by virtue of royal patronage. Signed pieces now tend to command exceptionally high prices, although many of the best articles were not stamped. Immigrant craftsmen from Germany, Italy and the Low Countries did not have to put their stamp on their work, but some of it is every bit as good as the native joinery and cabinetmaking. Noted French chairmakers included Jean-Baptiste Lebas, E. Meunier, Jean-Baptiste Tilliard and Pierre Nogaret of Lyons.

The essentially feminine flavour of French Rococo spread across Europe as far as Russia, where Count Bartolommeo Rastrelli, the Russian-born son of an Italian father, designed sofas so elaborately carved and gilded that they look more like picture frames than things to be sat on. In Poland there was equally assiduous copying of the French style by skilled craftsmen working on noblemen's estates. In Germany very ornate seat furniture, richly carved, painted and gilded, was produced for Frederick the Great in Berlin, while less ambitious productions were made for the palaces of less powerful princes. Names to note are those of the Hoppenhaupt brothers, the Spindler brothers, Johann August Nahl, Johann Melchior Kambli (a Swiss) and Abraham Roentgen, who spent some years in England before returning to Neuwied, where he established an important workshop in 1750.

ABOVE LEFT
Walnut chair, early 18th century. English influence is present in the basic structure and particularly in the shaping of the splat in the back, but a Germanic exaggeration of the Rococo style asserts itself in the asymmetrical carving of the cresting rail.
ABOVE RIGHT
Venetian armchair, first quarter of the 18th century, decorated with the Italian version of lacquer, and embellished with gilding. The Venetians used the term lacca *to describe all kinds of painted decoration that covered the entire surface of the woodwork.*

French armchair (fauteuil) in the fully developed Louis XV style, conceived as a continuous flow of gentle curves, the frame delicately carved and gilded, the upholstery in Beauvais tapestries made in 1737. It was the fashion to cover seat furniture with tapestries in pictorial designs, many of them executed by Boucher, between 1736 and 1756.

Fashionable furniture in the England of the 1740's, with which Roentgen must have become familiar, exhibited a marked Italian influence through the agency of William Kent, who designed sets of chairs and matching settees with cabriole legs, lion's-paw feet and elaborately fretted backs, either in solid mahogany or gilt, which are more Baroque than Rococo in feeling. These were outside the mainstream of the more homely English furniture, much of which continued the fairly simple Queen Anne style into the early and mid-Georgian period. The flowing lines, delicate C-scrolls, floral motifs and acanthus leaves which, in association with the cabriole leg and the long-lasting ball-and-claw foot, make up the repertoire of English Rococo, were closely followed in America by the Philadelphia school of designers, notably by Benjamin Randolph and William Savery. who studied the published designs of Ince and Mayhew, Robert Manwaring, Matthias Lock and H. Copland.

These last two were associated with Chippendale's book, *The Gentleman and Cabinet-Maker's Director*, the first edition of which appeared in 1754. It includes chairs 'in the French taste' and others with 'ribband' backs, as well as many with less ornate, pierced splats. A square or square-tapered Marlboro' leg is offered as an alternative to the cabriole, in association with some of these chair backs. The combination of fretted splat with square leg provided the basic pattern for any number of sensible, pleasing chairs, which were made in all qualities from the finest mahogany to the country version in oak or fruitwood with a wooden seat, not only in Britain but also in America, Germany, Scandinavia and Ireland. The Irish furniture of this time is remarkable for the lavish use of mahogany —

English settee in mahogany, mid 18th century. The ribbon back and the cabriole legs carved with opposing 'C' scrolls bring to perfection the English version of Rococo when handled by master craftsmen of Thomas Chippendale's eminence. The style was adopted, in somewhat modified form, in the English provinces and in America.

an expensive material—and for full-blooded carving.

Chairs in the 'Chinese Chippendale' style were made with backs latticed geometrically and cresting rails carved to represent little pagodas. England adopted this style with more enthusiasm than any other country, but it was attempted also in America and in Portugal. In France it was taken up by the distinguished chairmaker Georges Jacob. Similar designs were used in Berlin by Johann Michael Hoppenhaupt. All these were concerned with simulating oriental shapes in polished wood. The vogue for *chinoiseries* that spread across Europe at this time, and led to the creation of whole rooms in the oriental style in Austria, Scandinavia, Poland and Russia, was in fact more dependent on 'japanning' in imitation of lacquer than on the reproduction of actual shapes.

The Chippendale school also made a sophisticated version of the ladder or slat back which originated in Italy about 1500 and was widely distributed. The Bavarian version was gaily painted with flowers, while in Spain the rungs or slats were elaborately shaped. A tall-backed type with anything up to five slats, on robustly turned legs, was made of maple in the Delaware River valley from Colonial times onwards, while the slat-backed rocking chair was the best-known product of the Shakers, a sect established in Albany, New York, in 1774. In a different tradition—that of the Swiss 'auricular' type—is the German peasant chair with a solid seat, four splayed legs and a slab back shaped like a shield. This continued to be made by German settlers in America in the eighteenth century, who gave their names to a style misleadingly known as 'Pennsylvania Dutch'—'Dutch' being, in this context, a corruption of 'deutsch'.

An English mahogany side chair of the Chippendale period, c. 1760. The fretting of the splat in the back shows the influence of the Gothic revival.

American slatback rocking chair—the most popular of the many pieces of furniture made by the Shaker sect, from the last quarter of the 18th century until well into the 19th century.

Another type of country-made chair, which is found in many places and exhibits regional variations, is the 'comb' back in which the spindles are fixed into a solid cresting rail.

In many provincial areas—especially Normandy and parts of Germany—the curving lines of the Rococo were retained until the mid-nineteenth century, while in remote parts of Eastern Europe, such as the rural districts of Poland, craftsmen went on making furniture that was pure Gothic in form.

About mid-century the Chippendale school began to cater for the revival of interest in the 'Gothick' style, rendering the pointed arches, rose windows and clustered columns of medieval times in crisply carved mahogany. There does not seem to have been any attempt to fake the old oak of the true Gothic period—that was to come later, in the nineteenth century. The eighteenth-century Gothic style was taken up in a limited way by rural craftsmen. The Windsor chair, made in the forests of Buckinghamshire, and also in Philadelphia from about 1725 onwards, was essentially 'cottage' furniture, though it occasionally affected a fashionable quirk, such as cabriole legs in place of the usual turned ones, and—much more rarely—a Gothic arched back.

Many of these chairs successfully defied the rule that furniture should always be made of well-seasoned timber. Freshly cut 'green' wood had greater pliability than seasoned timber and could more easily be bent into shape for the hooped back, arms and 'crinoline' understretcher. The spindles and legs were turned on a lathe which was actually driven by the tension resulting from a cord attaching the treadle to the top of a growing sapling. English Windsors are usually a mixture of elm, beech, ash and—less commonly—yew with its beautifully curled grain. American Windsors are often more finely made than the English ones, with very slender spindles. They frequently have rush seats instead of the customary English elm, and lack the central splat with fretted wheel pattern found on the later British type. The wood used is most often hickory or maple, which was originally painted black or green.

Sophisticated society, however, by the mid-eighteenth century, had grown tired of Rococo frills and begun looking for a change. Its designers found inspiration in abundance in the architecture of ancient Rome. Madame de Pompadour's brother was sent to Rome in 1749 to study its antiquities, and was followed in the 1750's by an architect from Edinburgh, Robert Adam. Adam was particularly stimulated by meeting Giambattista Piranesi, who had published one of the very few Italian books of the period containing designs for furniture. These were based on what he imagined the furniture of ancient Rome to have been like—speculations which were proved remarkably accurate by subsequent excavations around the Bay of Naples. A distinctive Neapolitan chair of the late eighteenth century must owe something to local archaeology. It has an exceptionally wide seat and a geometrically pierced back, and is remarkably elegant. On the whole, however, the Italians were more interested in the sculptural achievements of their Roman ancestors, even in the field of furniture. The main impetus for the Neoclassical style of the second half of the eighteenth century sprang from the enthusiasm of the French and British designers. Known respectively as 'Louis XVI' and 'Adam', the two versions have a great deal in common. They formed the basis of an international style which replaced the flowers and shells of the Rococo with laurel wreaths and urns. Chair backs became oval, shield-shaped or square, with straight legs relieved by a gentle tapering, delicate fluting.

The style is seen at its best in the work of such makers as Jean-Baptiste Sené, a Parisian whose chairs can sometimes be recognized by his use of a thin spiral carved around the tapering leg. Most Louis XVI seat furniture conforms to the basic types—*fauteuil, bergère, canapé*—established in the previous reign, and even the replacement of the cabriole leg came about gradually, the carved decoration being the first clear expression of the new discipline, and the sense of richness persisting in the extensive use of gilding. France was relatively late in using mahogany to any great extent for chairs, but Jacob, one of the greatest makers of seat furniture, took to it with huge success.

Sweden produced a number of gilt armchairs with oval backs, rounded seats and fluted, vertical legs, which were very French in feeling but marked by a certain rigidity. Straight supports joined the back to the seat, whereas in the authentic French version slightly curved supports were normally used. It is in subtle details of this kind, too numerous to explore fully here, that specific regional differences are to be detected. An exceptionally severe adaptation of the Neoclassical chair, with a square back unadorned by carving, was produced in Copenhagen by Jens Brøtterup. He had been trained in London in the 1780's, with the encouragement of the director of the Danish Royal Furniture Emporium, who urged the adoption of Hepplewhite and Sheraton designs by his Danish craftsmen.

Ironically, neither George Hepplewhite nor Thomas Sheraton has left a single piece of furniture that can be attributed with confidence to the hands of either, although both were originally practical furniture makers. Unlike the French, the English eighteenth-century makers did not normally sign their work. Hepplewhite's designs were published in 1786 by his widow, two years after his death. His name is often associated with shield-back chairs, but it is interesting to note that designs for 15 variations of these appear in the third edition of his *Cabinet-Maker and Upholsterer's Guide*, published in 1794, as against 18 of the basically square form (which is popularly thought of as 'Sheraton') embellished with such devices as the wheatsheaf, the Prince of Wales's feathers and the 'Adam' urn.

Sheraton published *The Cabinet-Maker's and Upholsterer's Drawing Book* in four parts between 1791 and 1794. His designs are roughly contemporary with those of Hepplewhite, yet they show the change in taste that was occurring even in a few short years in favour of a lighter, more angular style for chairs. He illustrates only two with shield-backs as compared with 24 of the square type, which have vertical struts or lyre-shaped, delicately pierced splats set within them.

A much simplified version of this square-back chair with vertical struts, or sticks, became very popular for country furniture because the essentially sound principles of construction lent themselves to the limitations of the rural craftsmen, and to rugged usage in farmhouse and cottage. The type was often made in fruitwood, and occurs in widely distributed parts of Europe as well as in Britain.

Some remarkable chairs in cut steel, decorated with an inlay of softer metals, were made at Tula in Russia during the reign of Catherine the Great, but production ceased shortly after her death in 1796. They show the influence of Anglo-French Neoclassicism but retain an interestingly Russian flavour derived from the traditions of the Orthodox Church.

ABOVE
*English X-framed stools,
early 19th century,
closely modelled on an
ancient Roman curule
and characteristic of the
academic approach to
Neoclassical furniture
adopted by architects and
designers of the Empire
period.*
RIGHT
*Chair-back in the
American Federal style,
based on the designs of
Hepplewhite and
Sheraton. John Aitken
of Philadelphia made
chairs to this design for
George Washington in
1797.*

The War of Independence prevented both the publication in America of Robert Adam's designs and the importation of much European furniture. Peace was restored in 1783, however, and by 1790 the designs of Hepplewhite and Sheraton had become available and were being put to good use, notably by John Aitken of Philadelphia, John Seymour of Boston and Samuel McIntire of Salem, who regularly added a distinctive touch to his shield-back chairs by carving a trailing vine pattern down the front legs. New Hampshire produced the 'Martha Washington' chair with a high, stuffed back, low seat and open arms. During this period, known as 'Federal', a favourite New York side chair was square-backed, with a central carved motif of a draped urn within an arch. The most distinguished New York furniture maker was Duncan Phyfe, who abandoned his earlier style, closely modelled on Sheraton's designs, in favour of the 'Greek Revival'—the American phrase for the newest form of Neoclassicism. Jefferson actively encouraged the use of this style, which was derived from that of the *Directoire* then prevalent in France. Phyfe is especially remembered for his sabre-legged and X-framed chairs, and his Grecian-style, scroll-ended sofas; he also made much use of carved decoration at a time when the majority of American makers were favouring marquetry.

The French *Directoire* style was a conscious attempt, following the Revolution, to break with the grandeur and the gilt associated with the monarchy and replace it with something dignified and austere. Its most distinguished interpreter was Georges Jacob, who worked mainly in mahogany, producing chairs with latticed backs and legs of sabre shape or fashioned to resemble the hind leg of an animal with a cloven hoof. A personal touch of Jacob's—almost a trademark—is a marguerite often found carved on the seat rail of his chairs, a device which his two sons also used.

They became leading exponents of the Empire style which evolved from the *Directoire* during the Napoleonic period. At its most extreme, it was even grander and more heavily gilded than that of Louis XVI. Thronelike chairs had arms in the shape of winged lions or sphinxes, black and gold being a favourite combination. Square, architecturally inspired armchairs were produced by such men as P. Brion, who worked for the imperial court. Alongside these pompous types, between 1800 and 1815, a much more domestic, far less forbidding style developed, which has much in common with English Regency furniture of the same period.

This made use of mahogany, rosewood, and beech painted to simulate rosewood. Chairs with sabre or turned legs, scrolled arms and low backs made a feature of a horizontal bar carved like a rope, either as the cresting rail itself or placed halfway between cresting rail and seat. The cresting rail, if flat, was often decorated with inlaid brass, and a line or stringing of brass sometimes emphasized the flow of the back, seat and legs.

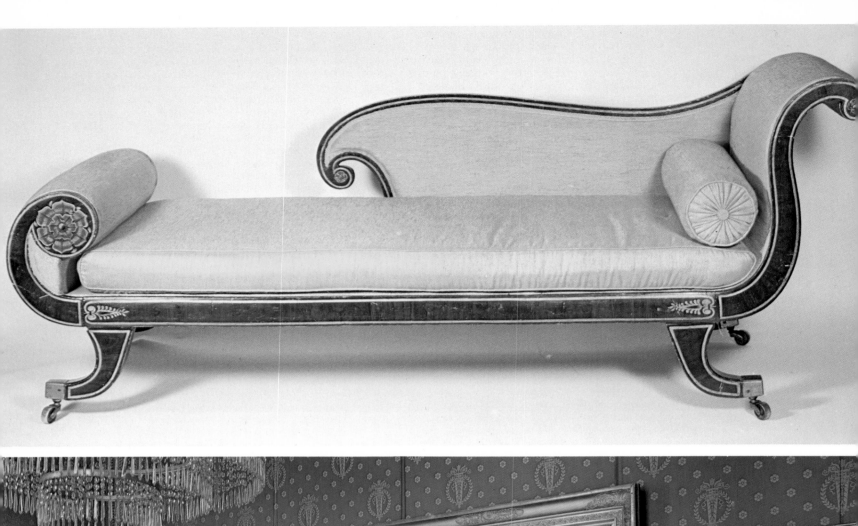

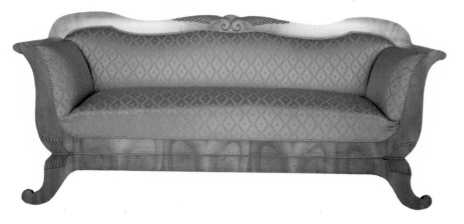

ABOVE
*Settee and two chairs, the
frames elaborately fretted
and carved in the style of
the 19th-century Rococo
revival, by John Belter.*
OPPOSITE ABOVE
*Scroll-ended couch, early
19th century. This
internationally popular
type was based, fairly
accurately, on the
couches painted on Greek
pottery. In America, the
period became designated
'Greek Revival'.*
OPPOSITE BELOW
*Neoclassical furniture in
the style of Schinkel.*
BELOW
*Sofa in the Biedermeier
style, German, early 19th
century. Pale-coloured
woods such as birch,
cherry and maple, known
collectively* bois clair, *were
popular during the period
1815–1830.*

The Italians, accustomed to a sculptural tradition, at first found it difficult to master the flat surfaces of mahogany and the rather rigid lines of the Empire style, and French craftsmen were brought to Florence to instruct the native craftsmen in the proper approach for furnishing the Palazzo Pitti.

A very heavy interpretation of the style was developed in Spain, where it is known as Fernandino. Chairs are supported on crossed horns of plenty, and sofas have legs formed like sphinxes or swans, massively carved and gilt. A style closer to the French original lasted in Portugal until that country was liberated from Napoleonic control. From then on, a simpler version of the style, much closer to the English Regency in spirit, continued to be popular until the 1830's.

The typical Danish home in the early nineteenth century did not normally reserve a room for dining. Meals were taken from a sofa table, and the sofa itself had cupboards placed at each end of it to hold china and cutlery. Though apparently confined to Denmark and Norway at that time, this combination was revived about half a century later in Russia.

During the Empire period, Andrei Voronikhin, in designing for the Pavlovsk Palace, had chairs made in the grandest Napoleonic style, gilded and tinted to look like patinated bronze. The predominant fashion in St Petersburg, for the less magnificent home, was a modified Empire style in which chairs combined features from the designs of Sheraton and Alphonse Jacob-Desmalter.

The outstanding Prussian designer of the Neoclassical period was Karl Friedrich Schinkel who was responsible both for the grand furniture in the Charlottenburg Palace, and for some very comfortable settees and chairs in a modified Greek or Gothic style. Similar in spirit were the products of Vienna—especially those of the manufacturer Josef Danhauser, who produced a wide range of furniture from 1804 to 1830 in the Empire style and the bourgeois Biedermeier version of it that followed. Originally *Biedermeier* was a derisory term, meaning 'would-be man of honour', applied to a whole school of thought compounded of idealism and resignation, which extolled the virtues of family life. The furniture—especially the seat furniture—expressed this mood by combining comfort with high-mindedness. Many features were taken over from the defunct Empire style—the arms of chairs and settees being shaped like swans' necks and heads with a realistic rendering of beaks and eyes. The rather sombre effect was lightened, very often, by the use of pale woods—particularly cherry and maple—known collectively as *bois clair*.

A Rococo revival, which began about 1830, brought forth the drawing room or 'parlour' suite. The chairs usually had balloon backs, either open or padded, and legs which sometimes were turned to heavy profiles and at others were shaped to an elegant version of the French cabriole leg. John Henry Belter, who emigrated from Germany to New York about 1840, produced some particularly elaborate examples of this revived Rococo style, the frames being intricately carved and pierced in the style of his native Württemberg. Rosewood, the most fashionable material, proved too brittle in its natural state for this treatment, so Belter patented a process for laminating layers of the wood (anything from three to 16), the grain of each layer lying at right angles to the next, thus providing a material that could be fretted and carved without any danger of its splitting.

RIGHT
English chairs typical of the early 19th century Gothic revival, c. 1820–1830. Heavier than the Gothic revival of the Chippendale period, the Regency version was popularized in George Smith's Household Furniture, *published in 1808 and again in 1826.*

BELOW LEFT
Irish oak dining chair, c. 1830, in a diluted version of the Neoclassical style comfortably adapted to middle class domesticity that became internationally current in the second quarter of the 19th century.

BELOW RIGHT
Chair made from the antlers of stags in mid 19th-century Germany. Many pieces of furniture were produced on the same principle. Hall stands were made from hunting trophies. The tusks of elephants were contrived to form tables and chairs, and even the animal's feet were made into umbrella stands.

In 1830 Michael Thonet began to experiment with the effect of steam pressure on birch rods so that they could be bent to make elaborately curved frames for chairs. At first these followed the Biedermeier style, but they soon developed into highly original creations, cheaply produced on an enormous scale and sold all over the world, making Thonet into one of the most successful furniture makers of all time. His chairs, though conceived quite simply as functional, commercial products, came to be praised by Le Corbusier and his disciples as the prototypes of the modern chair. Thonet's bentwood chairs were only one example of an admirable quality that characterized the nineteenth century: a readiness to experiment with materials which hitherto had been used, if at all, only in a limited way.

Papier-mâché, which had been used in Europe since the eighteenth century for trays, small boxes and trinkets, began to be used in mid-nineteenth-century England and America for furniture in which the deeply curved backs of chairs were moulded into shape and painted with flowers, landscapes, even portraits, with additional decoration in Rococo gilding and mother-of-pearl inlay. Quantities of garden chairs and seats were cast in iron at Coalbrookdale in England and Detroit, Michigan, while the metal-framed rocking chairs that first appeared at the Great Exhibition of 1851 in London were soon afterwards being copied in France and America. Spring steel was also used to provide resilient frames for the backs of fully upholstered chairs, although most chairs of this type, as well as Chesterfield settees, were wood-framed with coiled metal springs.

Buffalo horns in America, and stag antlers in Germany and Scotland, were skilfully assembled to form rather barbaric-looking thrones, which expressed, in an extreme way, an urge to use natural materials imaginatively. Interest in the Gothic revival was also widespread, especially in England, where as early as 1808, George Smith, a practical cabinetmaker, had published a book of designs that had an international impact, and in which many cathedral-like chairs and hall seats with pointed and cusped arches appear.

Rocking chair in bentwood produced by Michael Thonet, the Austrian manufacturer, about 1850. Thonet's products were intended to be functional and commercial, but achieved artistry.

BELOW LEFT
English oak armchair designed by C. F. A. Voysey, whose designs for furniture were executed from about 1886 to 1910. His work influenced Art Nouveau design in the rest of Europe, most of which he disliked intensely.

BELOW RIGHT
Walnut armchair designed by Louis Majorelle of Nancy, a leading exponent of French Art Nouveau. His best period was from 1900 to 1906; his favourite motif, a lily.

In Victorian Britain the Arts and Crafts Movement tried to put the clock back by reviving hand craftsmanship based on medieval forms, while in New York the firm of Sypher and Company marketed a glamorized version of the primitive chairs made by the early settlers. Cracow was the centre of a revival of peasant traditions, based on Polish folk art, known as the Zakopane style. In Russia Prince Savva Ivanovich Mamontov attempted to do the same for the native culture by establishing workshops on his estate where chairs with arched, fretted backs were produced.

Curiously, what emerged from these well-meant, conscious attempts to get back to the grass roots of national idioms was, with a few exceptions, not at all the idealized simplicity that their originators had in mind, but a number of highly sophisticated styles now known collectively as Art Nouveau. This ranges from the built-in 'inglenook' seating, based on the primitive farmhouse settle, designed by M. H. Baillie Scott, to the chairs with exaggeratedly high backs and absurdly low seats made by Charles Rennie Mackintosh in Britain; from the slightly macabre designs of Antonio Gaudi, in Spain, which owe something to the auricular style in that they based chair legs, arms and backs on the forms of human flesh and bones, to the sinuous lines employed by Louis Tiffany in America, and by Louis Majorelle and Eugène Vallin in France, Victor Horta in Belgium and Henri van de Velde, a Belgian who settled in Germany. These designers used the winding stalks of growing plants as the motif for carved mouldings that accentuated the lines of the chairs, earning the genre the unkind epithet of 'macaroni'. In Vienna a new group was founded, known as the Sezession, which broke away from this botanical main stem of Art Nouveau to cultivate their own ideas for more functional furniture in the spirit of the earlier reform movement. About 1900, Art Nouveau mannerisms were applied to a wide range of commercially

produced furniture, giving a fashionable touch to the bourgeois preference for diluted Neoclassicism. This had resulted in a vogue for chairs and prim little settees with thin, tapering legs made of mahogany with Art Nouveau flowers inlaid, formally, in satin-wood—Sheraton gone to seed but achieving a certain weedy elegance.

In the early 1900's, at about the time that work-shops for functional furniture were being established in Vienna, the American architect Frank Lloyd Wright began to design 'constructivist' chairs com-posed of boards mounted on a framework of laths. Gerrit Rietveld of Utrecht followed this during World War I with a deceptively simple-looking chair in which the frame was constructed of lengths of batten, screwed together without recourse to traditional methods of jointing, with the back made of one solid board and the seat from another. The frame was painted black, while the seat and back are in vivid colours.

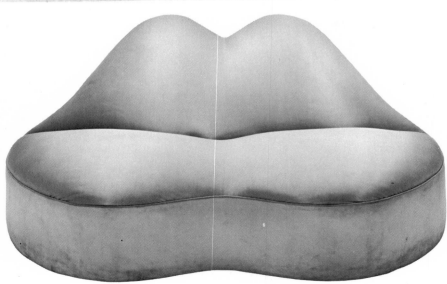

A revolutionary advance in chair design was effected in the 1920's, first by Mies van der Rohe and shortly after by Breuer, both of whom used tubular metal to construct cantilevered frames which dispensed entirely with rear legs and with additional springing, and yet remained stable and resilient. These were the prototypes of all the tubular metal furniture that was to follow, and also of the cantilevered chairs which were developed in Finland using laminated birch. Although the principle of lamination was known and used in the eighteenth and nineteenth centuries, it had never before been exploited for this purpose.

Some of the tubular metal chairs made in the period between 1925 and the outbreak of World War II fall into the category of Art Deco, although by definition purely functional types ought really to be excluded. More truly characteristic of the style are the fully upholstered armchairs and settees with wide, bold arms placed like huge slabs alongside seat and back, and upholstered in fabrics of brightly contrasting colours and abstract design. Sometimes the arms are wheel-like, sometimes square with facings of walnut at their fronts. Although functional in the sense that they can be lounged in, their aim was to offer a feeling of luxury rather than to provide real comfort. Because they were designed without sufficient regard for the need to support the human frame scientifically, they allowed the user to feel prosperous and pampered, but left him with an aching back.

Metal in either tubular or strip form was used by Mies, Le Corbusier and others to produce a range of seat furniture which was carefully thought out to provide real comfort and survive hard use. Mies's 'Barcelona' chair of 1929 had an X-shaped frame which may have owed something to the folding deck chair, but its back and seat comprised two cushions which rested directly on the metal frame. Two years earlier Le Corbusier had created a chaise longue designed to support the human body in a semirecumbent position, and adjustable to varied angles at the user's choice. A similar principle has been applied with some success to a number of contemporary chairs and couches.

Following the success of his shell-shaped chair

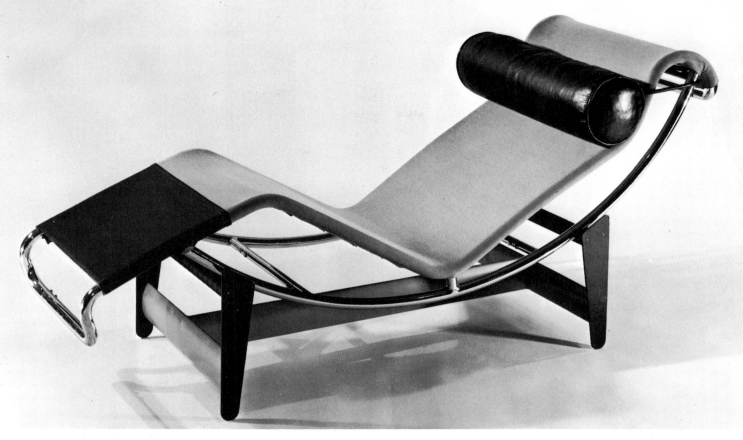

ABOVE
Chaise longue designed by Le Corbusier (Charles-Edouard Jeanneret) in association with Charlotte Perriand and Pierre Jeanneret, 1927, and made of tubular steel. It is adjustable and gives priority to comfort.

LEFT
Lounge chair and ottoman (footrest) designed by Charles Eames in 1957. Eames is rightly regarded as of major importance, but like many of the great designers of the past, he has been imitated by lesser men and his name is often applied recklessly to a debased style that might be described as 'reproduction contemporary'.
BELOW
Settee and chair with tubular steel frames by Vono, c. 1972. The clinical flavour of modern metal furniture is toned down by the comfortable upholstery.

mounted on metal rods which took a prize in 1940 and went into full production in 1946, the American designer Charles Eames went on to design what is now known as the 'Eames' chair—a dining chair with a moulded plywood seat and back, also mounted on metal rods. In 1957 Eames produced a chair in laminated rosewood on a centre stem from which four feet splayed outwards. This chair and its accompanying footstool have been much imitated and to have them in the office has become the symbol of success for today's executive class.

Chippendale called his book *The Gentleman and Cabinet-marker's Director*. For 'gentleman' read 'executive', and his title would become immediately intelligible in contemporary life. Le Corbusier designed 'equipment' as part of his 'machine for living'. The best modern chairs manage to satisfy both designers' requirements—to combine the functions of the traditional place of honour, and the practical seat. In evolutionary terms, it took man a long time to learn to stand up straight. In practical terms it has taken him a long time to learn to sit down in comfort.

THE CHEST

The first wooden receptacle used for storing precious possessions was almost certainly a vertical piece of built-in furniture—a hollow tree which, if struck by lightning, became horizontal and movable. Dragged to a convenient spot near the cave man's home, the tree trunk became the travelling trunk. The demand for hollow trees struck by lightning soon exceeding the supply, someone hit on the idea of hollowing out a log by his own efforts, using fire and flints. Dug-out chests made on this principle but using steel tools in place of flints were still being produced in some rural areas of Europe—Wales, for example—as late as the seventeenth century.

As early as 1500 BC the Egyptians were constructing chests, some with domed lids, their carcases mitred and dovetailed at the corners or jointed by mortise and tenon, their surfaces veneered in ivory and ebony or painted to imitate them. The Greeks and Romans made elaborate chests shaped like sarcophagi, thereby setting a precedent for chests to look like coffins which has lasted down to comparatively modern times, the trades of undertaker and house furnisher being closely linked. The Etruscans used both wood and bronze to make small circular chests. Byzantine workmen made them in many sizes and types, some of them with framed construction and elaborate decoration in painting or inlay in ivory and precious metals.

In Europe during the early Middle Ages the chest took pride of place as the most important piece of furniture in the house. It could handily hold the family valuables and be loaded onto a cart when a marauding enemy came uncomfortably close—as, only too often, he did. In the thirteenth century chests in Southern Europe particularly—less commonly in the north—were carved in Romanesque style with rounded arches supported on columns. Construction of these was on a massive scale, the horizontal boards forming the carcase being 'housed' or slotted into the uprights or 'stiles' at the four corners.

The same method of construction continued into the Gothic period in Northern Europe, but decoration varied regionally. The typical Westphalian type relied for its decoration on the very large strap hinges and strengthening bands made of iron. The French were fond of scrolled ironwork all over the lid and front, while the English preference was for simple 'chip' carving—a formal design, such as a roundel borrowed from sacred architecture, chipped out of the surface with a chisel with little attempt at rendering it in relief. Linenfold patterns were carved on some, and a few had figures of knights.

Italy, however, had never taken cordially to the Gothic style. The classical tradition remained so strong, despite destruction and neglect, that when, in the fifteenth century, the Renaissance brought the revival of old arts and the development of new ones, some of the really grand *cassoni*, ordered by rich patrons as dower chests for their daughters, were painted by fine artists, the subjects being either Christian saints or the gods and goddesses of Olympus.

The *cassone* or chest often followed the outline of the Roman sarcophagus, curving inwards at the base and supported on lion's-paw feet. Decorative styles were sometimes blended with each other, the carving of the front combining Romanesque arcading with a Gothic-style family crest at the centre, contained within a classical laurel wreath. Sixteenth-century *cassoni* continued to be made in both

curvilinear and rectilinear forms, and both were used as the basis of the *cassapanca* with box seat, ornate back and arms. In this form it was the forerunner of both the sophisticated settee and its country cousin, the settle. The *cassapanca* traditionally stood in the entrance hall of the palazzo, with the owner's wealth locked inside it and an armed guard sitting—even sleeping—on it. It had the added advantage—unlike some other articles of furniture designed for the display of wealth—of being very inpressive, even when empty.

Important changes in the methods of constructing the chest spread northwards through Europe during the first half of the sixteenth century. The massive Gothic chest, made of thick boards in huge styles, was heavy to move, especially when full. A lighter but crude alternative was the nailing of planks to a pair of slab ends, with no vertical stiles. A refinement of this type used dovetailed joints in place of nails—a method which continued in use, in widely scattered areas of the world, until the eighteenth century, and hence should not be taken as conclusive evidence of sixteenth-century origin. In Bermuda, where a variety of European adventurers arrived as colonists early in the seventeenth century, an interesting version was made in cedar, in which the joiner varied the cutting of the exposed dovetails to form an intricate pattern. Further decoration, apparently

derived from Italian sources, was provided by 'scratch' carving—the design being lightly cut in continuous lines with a chisel or similar tool, with no attempt at modelling in relief.

Another method, known since early times but which was slow in being applied to the chest in Northern Europe, was panelled construction. In this a strong framework was joined at the angles by mortise and tenon, secured by dowel pins; the front, the back and usually the lid too were divided into two, three or four equal areas by vertical stiles similarly jointed to the rails above and below; and into this framework panels were fitted, their edges bevelled to allow a neat but relatively loose fit that guarded against any shrinkage in the timber. Though still very substantial, this type of chest was lighter and more manageable than earlier styles, and was produced in some areas until about 1750.

In medieval Scandinavia, where the woodworking skills of the Viking shipwrights had been handed down, a rather different method was followed. Turned posts took the place of the flat stiles at the corners, with the horizontal boards housed into them, and decoration was provided by a row of turned spindles set between the bottom of the box and the understretchers. The top is often sloped to form a desk for reading and writing.

Another method of decorating the chest was with

OPPOSITE ABOVE
French Gothic chest in oak, late 15th or early 16th century. The lockplate is characteristic of fine French ironwork of the period.

OPPOSITE BELOW
Early 16th-century oak chest, Netherlands, carved in the Renaissance style with pilasters flanking panels carved with portrait medallions.

BELOW
Detail of an English Gothic oak chest, late 16th to early 17th century, showing the front housed into the vertical style. It is elaborately carved with motifs typical of the period. Such decoration on English chests was usually less ambitious than that on French equivalents.

76

ABOVE
*Casket made in Augsburg
c. 1570. The columns
are of rock crystal,
skilfully carved, and the
elaborate inlaid decoration
employs a variety of
semi-precious stones.
German craftsmen such
as Peter Flötner and
Lienhart Strohmeier
adopted the Italian
Renaissance style with
enthusiasm. Augsburg
and Nuremberg were the
centres in Southern
Germany for furniture
decorated with inlay.*

inlay or intarsia work, in woods of contrasting colours, metals and shells—a technique practised with particular skill at Nuremberg in the sixteenth century, often on themes of landscapes with buildings. In Britain this type is known as a 'Nonesuch' chest because of several examples which are supposed to depict the palace of that name, built by Henry VIII. They were probably imported from Germany or made by immigrant craftsmen. Light-coloured woods such as box were inlaid into a darker ground of solid walnut in order to achieve brilliant effects.

The term 'German' is used here not to define a sovereign state, but rather to suggest a cultural identity based on language, which has long been common to the peoples in what is now known as Germany and also in Austria, and parts of Switzerland and the Low Countries. Despite the common cultural heritage, however, there were distinct differences in the furniture of these areas. The further south the stronger the Italian influence, and Renaissance ideas were absorbed there earlier than in the countries to the north, where Gothic traditions lingered longer. This principle applies to the

materials used as well as to the ornament—the first dictating, to some extent, the choice of the second. Pine, readily available in the alpine countries, lent itself to painted decoration, while oak and a certain amount of walnut, carved or inlaid, were more usual in the north.

In the south, Islamic decoration of a formal kind, which deliberately avoided portrayal of the human figure, was introduced to Spain by the Moors and remained a powerful influence there long after Moorish rule had ended. Many motifs which are usually regarded as essentially European actually sprang from this source; for example, before the conquest of Sicily by the Normans, the pointed arch of Gothic architecture had already arrived there directly from the Middle East.

This *mudéjar* style, inherited from the Moorish occupation of Spain, is seen in much Spanish furniture. One of its forms, sometimes found on the panels of chests, is the inlaying of arabesques in ivory into a walnut ground. Silver was also used for this purpose, and the power of Spain, which was at its height in the sixteenth century, is clearly reflected in the magnificent furniture made for the

BELOW
*Detail of Augsburg
casket, showing the
inlaid decoration.*

BOTTOM
*Early 17th-century chest,
South German or Italian,
with armorial bearings in
light-coloured woods
inlaid into solid walnut.
Italian and Southern
German furniture often
influenced each other.*

aristocracy. Chests in the typical well-to-do household were modelled on the Italian *cassone* and embellished with classical columns, rounded arches and caryatids—architectural supports with their upper halves formed as human figures. Even the undersides of lids were decorated with painting or carving. In peasant communities the Spanish Gothic version of the chest persisted into the seventeenth century. Such chests were of boarded construction, the front and back being dovetailed to the ends and the whole of the front covered with chip carving. The end boards projected beyond the front to form feet. The late sixteenth-century iron box with elaborate locking devices popularly known as an 'Armada chest' was not, in fact, Spanish but German. Spanish influence extended to parts of the Netherlands, to Portugal and to Spanish colonies in the New World, for furniture in the Spanish style was being made in Mexico before 1600. Very little Portuguese furniture made earlier than that date has survived, because so much has been destroyed by wars and earthquakes, but what there is suggests that it was closely modelled on Spanish and Italian types.

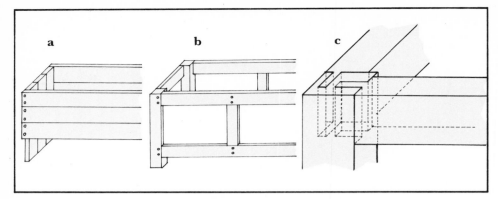

ABOVE
a. *Plank construction. A crude method which persisted well into the 18th century. The front of the chest is nailed to the ends with iron nails;*
b. *Framed construction. The chest is made by joining a frame together by means of mortise and tenon joints, secured by wooden dowel pins. Panels are held within the framework;*
c. *Diagram of mortise and tenon joints. Tongues at the end of the horizontal parts of the frame are let into cavities cut into the uprights.*
RIGHT
Carved portrait medallion of the type known as 'Romayne work', in the Northern European Renaissance style, sixteenth century. A fragment, a panel of this type, is now a collector's piece in its own right.

English carpenters took to the panelled construction readily enough, but approached Renaissance decoration rather more cautiously, adding certain features of it to the existing Gothic. Traditional linenfold and chip-carved roundels appear on panels within a framework decorated with 'strapwork'—the very flat carving of hook like scrolls which was derived through the Netherlands from Spanish-Moorish sources.

The popular term 'coffer' is applied on both sides of the Atlantic to conventionally shaped chests, but purists insist that it should properly be reserved for the type with a domed or arched lid—'coved' or 'coffered'—also known as an 'ark'. This shape, familiar in Holland, Scandinavia and the North of England from very early times, probably came about when the maker of a primitive dug-out chest first sliced off a length of the tree trunk and then used it, with its natural curve more or less untrimmed, as a lid for his laboriously hollowed-out log. In farming communities this lid was also hollowed out and used for carrying the grain that was stored in the chest. More sophisticated versions for domestic use were made in the seventeenth century, with their arklike shape emphasized their mouldings.

In the Netherlands large chests of panelled construction were enriched with fluted columns superimposed on the stiles, and the panels were frequently carved with Romayne work—portrayals of classical gods and goddesses or profiles of the owner and his wife disguised as Greeks and Romans. About 1580, designs for furniture with Renaissance ornamentation were published by Hans Vredeman de Vries, providing patterns for Dutch, Flemish, German, Swedish and even English craftsmen. He was probably familiar with the French Mannerist

BELOW
Said to have been made in memory of Erasmus for his heir, Bonifazius Amerbach, this chest in ash and lime was made

in Basle about 1539 by Jacob Steiner and Veltin Redner. The Romayne work panel on the left has a medallion portrait of Erasmus at its centre.

designs of Jacques Androuet Ducerceau and Hugues Sambin, which appeared in 1550 and 1572 respectively, employing the human figure and grotesque animals as subjects for the woodcarver.

In Italy the Mannerist habit of depicting figures in isolation was replaced in the seventeenth century by the much more complex treatment accorded them by the Baroque style. The whole front of the *cassone* became an area to be enriched by inlaid designs of armorial bearings or by carving in depth of classical figures, foliage and scrollwork, framed in heavy mouldings. The skilful use of mouldings, not merely as a form of framing or finishing a raw edge, but as a means of decoration applied to the surface, became very popular in the seventeenth century. Cut into short lengths, their ends mitred to form angles, they were used to make up geometrical patterns based on Spanish-Moorish forms. This kind of arrangement is often seen in conjunction with split-baluster turning. To achieve this effect, two lengths of wood—sometimes matching, sometimes of contrasting colours—were lightly glued together so that they could be turned as one, on the lathe, to a baluster shape. The joint was then split open, leaving two strips, each with a flat side that could be glued to the surface of the piece.

This use of applied mouldings and baluster turnings became widespread in Europe and towards the end of the seventeenth century in America also. It forms an important element in the style known in the English-speaking world as 'Jacobean'—a term which, though historically imprecise, is useful for describing the relatively severe furniture that continued to be made after the more florid 'Restoration' became fashionable in Britain (but not in America) about 1660.

ABOVE
Seventeenth-century English dough chest, the top domed or 'arked'. The lids of such chests were often detachable and used for carrying grain, flour or dough.

BELOW
Italian cassone, *early 17th century, carved in the transitional style that bridges Renaissance and Baroque, the rather rigid, disciplined Mannerist style.*

Early American chest, c. 1675–1700. A well-known group of such chests from Connecticut are attributed to the hand of Peter Blin of Wethersfield. They are distinguished by very flat carving of tulips and sunflowers. Often they are decorated with split baluster turnings and fitted with oval wooden knobs known as 'turtleback'. They are based on English and Dutch models, but have a flavour of their own.

The Bible box was a small chest, popular in Holland, Britain and America from about 1650 to 1750. Sometimes it was mounted on a stand and, like the larger chest, often carved with a date and the initials of the owner. It was a valued possession, which held the family Bible and other documents of importance. The full-scale chests were equally prized. Many of them must have held the treasured possessions of early settlers on their voyage out to America. There, later, they would be copied with touches of originality. American-made chests dating from about 1675 have survived, some with applied split-turnery, some carved, some painted. The woods used were oak, pine and other locally grown timber. A few of the makers are known by name: Joseph Brown, Edward Dear, Thomas Dennis and William Searle of Ipswich, Massachusetts; the Allis and Belding families, and Peter Blin, in the Connecticut River valley, who favoured carved, floral decoration.

Not all these American chests were of simple box construction. Some were fitted, wholly or partly, with drawers. It had been the practice in Europe since the late sixteenth century to fit small drawers inside dome-topped travelling chests. From early

in the seventeenth century onwards, it became usual to place one long drawer, or two small ones set side by side, in the base of the domestic chest. This novelty became a minor status symbol, and some chests were made with one or two practical drawers at the bottom, the rest of the front being decorated with mouldings to simulate the appearance of more drawers. The chest which combines a box above with drawers below is known as a 'mule chest' because it is a hybrid; but the mule is very rarely fertile, whereas the mule chest proved to be a highly potent development. More and more drawers were added, until they occupied the entire carcase.

The chest of drawers had been born.

The chest of drawers In the late seventeenth century the method of making a chest of drawers changed. The original method, adapted from the construction of the boxlike chest, had been to make a frame and set panels in the ends. This was discarded by the cabinetmaker, whose craft had come to be regarded as distinct from, and in certain ways superior to, that of the joiner. The main difference lay in the cabinetmaker's ability to use veneers,

Chest of drawers in the Anglo-Dutch style, c. 1670–1700, with marquetry decoration. It was more usual for chests of this period to have bun feet. Bracket feet were often later replacements.

while the joiner worked only in the solid wood. The line of demarcation between the trades was often vague, and varied from country to country, depending on the way in which the guilds were organized and the extent to which they co-operated or disputed with each other. In the case of a chest of drawers, the work was often divided. The joiner would construct the carcase in a solid wood such as oak or pine, or a combination of the two, making the ends with boards glued together, edge to edge, and joined by the drawer dividers. He would use thick dovetails which, along with the ends, the top and the flush drawer fronts, would later be veneered by the cabinetmaker.

The close association between Holland and Britain led to an Anglo-Dutch style, which lasted from about 1660 to 1700. The tops, fronts and sometimes the ends of chests of drawers were treated as though they were artists' canvases, with floral decoration inspired by Dutch flower painting, or 'seaweed' designs, in marquetry of variously coloured woods inlaid into ovals of ebony against a ground of walnut or laburnum. Such changes did not occur overnight, however, and there are many

Two English oak bible boxes, the lower one on a stand and dated 1700. It is also carved with the initials 'H + S', suggesting a marriage between 'H' and 'S' at that date.

83

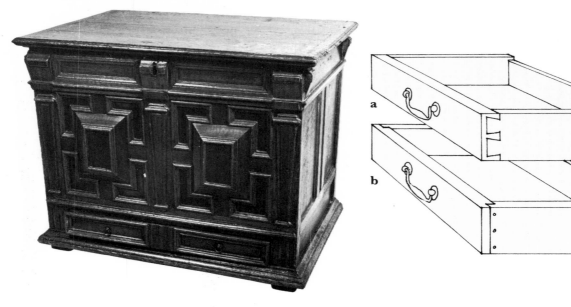

RIGHT
Jacobean oak mule chest fitted with drawers below and decorated with split turnery; English, 17th century.

FAR RIGHT
a. *Drawer constructed with dovetails, used on better quality furniture, especially in England, from c. 1700 onwards;*
b. *Drawer constructed with shoulder joint, used on cruder types of English furniture and on some sophisticated pieces in other countries, especially Italy, until the 19th century.*

84

LEFT
Seventeenth-century chest of drawers in the Jacobean style, with heavily moulded drawer fronts, c. 1670. The chest of drawers had developed from the mule chest.

BELOW RIGHT
Early 18th-century English bachelor chest of drawers, veneered in walnut. The fold-over top is hinged at the front and when extended forwards is supported on sliding supports known as 'lopers'.

RIGHT
Jacobean chest of drawers dated 1678. The arrangement consists of a shallow drawer above; then a deep drawer disguised as doors, with a panel inlaid with parquetry to create a sense of perspective; below, a pair of doors which conceal more drawers. English, with marked Dutch and Spanish influence, this piece is partly veneered with yew, sycamore, ebony and other woods.

instances of drawers made from about 1650 to 1680 in the Jacobean style, with fronts which were both heavily moulded and veneered. Brass pear-drop handles replaced the small wooden knob. Walnut remained the fashionable wood in Holland and Britain until about 1725. Turned, bun-shaped feet were usual until the bracket foot began to replace them in the 1690's, while brass handles with loops and backplates replaced the pear-drop design. During the early eighteenth century the English chest of drawers continued to be rectilinear in shape, the use of marquetry gradually subsided, and the emphasis was increasingly placed on good craftsmanship, well-chosen walnut veneers and such optional extras as the brushing slide or the extending top—the latter type being known as a 'bachelor's' chest.

Construction of the drawer was at first fairly crude; the front was attached to the sides by a shouldered joint (see opposite) which was secured with nails. This method persisted in country districts until the nineteenth century, when machined dovetailing became fairly general. On better-quality furniture hand dovetailing was used in most countries well before 1700, but its execution varied in quality from country to country. Until about 1690 the drawer sides were grooved to slide on runners attached to the interior of the carcase, but after 1700 this method was abandoned and the runners were set instead below the drawers until the 1960's when the side-runner was revived for certain items of mass-produced furniture. It is a useful rule of thumb that, until about 1750, the grain of the wood in drawer bottoms, on English furniture especially, ran from back to front, except in the case of very small drawers, and thereafter from side to side. However, there are many exceptions to this principle, especially in Southern European furniture, and no piece should be rejected as 'late' on this kind of evidence alone.

The Anglo-Dutch chest of drawers was often given importance by mounting it on a stand. The earlier version of the stand had bun feet or short spiral legs, while the later design stood on higher legs turned with an inverted cup above a tapering shaft and joined near floor level by flat stretchers. The stand usually had a shaped 'apron' and was fitted with three small drawers. Most drawer fronts were edged with cock beading—a much diminished version of the heavy mouldings it replaced—and banded with strips of veneer, the grain arranged in opposing diagonals to provide the effect called herringbone. Dutch chests on stands often have a double-dome top to the upper stage, but this feature is much less common in English examples. After about 1700, this 'William-and-Mary' style was modified into the 'Queen Anne', mainly by substituting cabriole legs for the turned variety.

BELOW LEFT
American highboy in mahogany with bonnet top, the stand having cabriole legs, c. 1750. The type is known in Britain as a tallboy or chest on stand.

BELOW RIGHT
American highboy made for Commodore Joshua Loring, c. 1740–1750, by John Pimm of Boston. Japanning in imitation of oriental lacquer was a Boston speciality, and this fine decoration was probably carried out by Thomas Johnson.

Both styles were followed very successfully in America and survived there longer than they did in Britain. There were important centres of production in Pennsylvania, New Jersey, the Connecticut River valley and Newport, Rhode Island. Distinctive national and even regional characteristics asserted themselves. Connecticut produced chests of drawers with scalloped edges, the nearest European equivalent of which was found in Portugal. The 'highboy' or chest on stand in the American William-and-Mary style has turned legs which are slimmer than either the Dutch or the English, and when it takes the form of a chest-on-chest (a double chest of drawers), it often displays a sunburst effect, inlaid or carved, at the base of the lower stage and at the top of the upper. The 'bonnet top'—a refinement of the Dutch double dome—is also characteristic of American craftsmanship in the early eighteenth century. The main influences were Anglo-Dutch,

with colourful additions provided by German immigrants in Pennsylvania, who painted some of their chests with lively heraldic designs, and by lacquering in the oriental style—a technique practised chiefly in Boston. French influence, which greatly affected the design of chests of drawers on the European continent during the first half of the eighteenth century, was hardly felt in America.

The French chest of drawers or commode originated in the 1660's as a basically rectilinear object, rounded at the front corners, massive in form, with three or four drawers reaching almost to the floor, the thickness of their fronts projecting beyond the carcase. In its more luxurious form it was veneered with walnut and ebony decorated with marquetry. The master cabinetmaker André-Charles Boulle (or Buhl) introduced a sarcophagus shape, a serpentine curve to the front, and, a little later, a type with a two-drawer depth standing on legs. He is better

known for the decorative technique to which he gave his name—'Boullework'—the inlaying of arabesque and *chinoiserie* designs of great complexity, cut out in sheet brass, into a ground of transparent tortoiseshell which, because of an underlay of coloured mica, appears red or occasionally green. The serpentine curve was developed by Charles Cressent between 1700 and 1735 (the period known stylistically as the *Régence*) on the vertical as well as the lateral plane, until it achieved the full *bombé* (swollen) shape on the ends, as well as the front, of the commode.

In France the *bombé* commode became increasingly elegant, the curving line continuing down the leg to the foot and emphasized by Rococo mounts with handles to match in gilded bronze (ormolu), made by a lengthy and costly process of casting, chiselling and gilding. The most usual decoration was mar-

quetry work in pale-coloured woods, some artificially stained with bright colours, with floral and *chinoiserie* motives as the favourite themes. In the Louis XV period these were executed with more gaiety than had been the custom during the *Régence*. But strangely enough the total effect was often marred when the handles and escutcheons were fitted with little regard for the design of the marquetry; only a few of the most distinguished cabinet-makers, men such as Martin Carlin, Jacques Dubois and Bernard van Risen Burgh, took the trouble to ensure that the placing of the mounts was consistent with the whole. This was especially important in the finest commodes, which were made with the drawer fronts overlapping and concealing the dividing rails so that their fronts presented an apparently uninterrupted surface which could be treated pictorially as a single area.

Besides pictorial marquetry and the more geometric parquetry these pieces were sometimes painted with *fêtes galantes* in the manner of Antoine Watteau and François Boucher, using a special varnish—*vernis Martin*—named after the four brothers who invented and patented it. Commodes were also painted, wholly or in part, in imitation of oriental lacquer.

Whatever the method of decoration, the commode was very much a status symbol in France, occupying the most important position in the room, and the skills of the finest native and foreign cabinetmakers were called upon to embellish it. The names of most of these men are recorded, and are often found stamped, followed by the letters JME (*juré des menuisiers et ébénistes*, indicating membership of the guild of joiners and cabinetmakers) in a fairly unobtrusive place, often in the unpolished wood below the marble top. This was the most usual finish in France, but not always in those other countries where the *bombé* commode was also favoured.

Spanish craftsmen were particularly influenced by the French designers and went on producing richly decorated commodes in the early Boulle style for many years after they had ceased to be fashionable in France. A less ornate type of Spanish commode had more in common with the provincial French version; it was constructed in the solid wood

without veneers and decorated with carving, with a front that was serpentine in shape rather than *bombé*. Similar types continued to be made in the French country districts and many other parts of Europe until the end of the eighteenth century, retaining something of the Rococo spirit long after it had been rejected in the cities. The Portuguese version of the commode is relatively tall, with four drawers, serpentine-fronted and canted at the corners. A somewhat similar shaping of the front is found much further north, in Norway and Denmark, where the traditional chest of drawers was brightly painted and stood on a separate stand, often gilded, the legs carved realistically to represent the legs of animals.

The Germans, though they provided Paris with some first-class cabinetmakers, tended towards heaviness and an exaggeration of the *bombé* bulge in commodes made for their own use. Though their guilds insisted on high standards, members were not required by law to sign their work. Some of the leading craftsmen at the main centres are, however, known by name: Franz Anton Schlott and Ferdinand Hund of Bamberg, Carl Maximilian Mattern of Würzburg, Martin Schumacher of Ansbach. Schumacher was one of the few Germans who, as a result of English influence, began working in mahogany earlier than 1750. Matthäus Eberhard Müller of

OPPOSITE ABOVE
Eighteenth-century French provincial commode. Pieces of this type were made in solid oak, walnut or fruitwood in the country districts of France, Germany and Spain, and were often finely carved.
OPPOSITE BELOW
Highly elaborate German commode made by Heinrich Spindler for Frederick the Great, c. 1765. Veneered in tortoiseshell, this very ornate Prussian piece is loaded in ormolu, probably the work of the Swiss craftsman, Johann Melchior Kambli.

LEFT
A fine French 18th-century ormolu mount, cast in bronze, chiselled and gilded by amalgamating pure gold with mercury. The mercury was then evaporated, and the mount burnished. Makers of ormolu had their own guild in Paris. In Britain, a similar process was followed by Matthew Boulton. From about 1820, cheaper processes that dispensed with real gold came into general use, and quality declined.

89

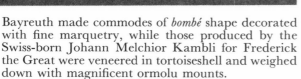

Bayreuth made commodes of *bombé* shape decorated with fine marquetry, while those produced by the Swiss-born Johann Melchior Kambli for Frederick the Great were veneered in tortoiseshell and weighed down with magnificent ormolu mounts.

Swedish designers employed the *bombé* shape, but always with three drawers which were often divided by strips of brass. The standard of Swedish workmanship was extremely high, with particular attention given to the construction of the interior, and the ormolu handles were sometimes delicate to the point of fragility.

The Dutch, who became very devoted to the *bombé* shape, often veneered the top and decorated it with marquetry to match the front, or even concentrated the decoration on the top, leaving the front relatively plain. Much good, plain Dutch furniture of the eighteenth century was reveneered and decorated with coarse marquetry in the late nineteenth and early twentieth centuries, unfairly giving the earlier work a bad name.

Italian craftsmen, once their magnificent *cassoni* had ceased to be fashionable, seem to have treated the commode as an opportunity for light-hearted experiment, and the Venetians in particular produced some absurd but charming confections with curving contours, cheerfully painted with flowers on green, blue and ivory-coloured grounds. The structural work shows a sad decline from the high standards of the previous century, but in the late eighteenth century some outstandingly fine marquetry decoration is found on commodes that are attributed with more enthusiasm than accuracy to Giuseppe Maggiolini, who was renowned for favouring a broad horizontal area at the centre front for portrait medallions of Roman emperors, flanked by scrolls and cornucopias. The general lack of information about the identity of the craftsmen in Italy at this time is also responsible for some rather wild attributions of anything carved and painted in the Neoclassical style to G. M. Bonzanigo of Turin.

By the 1760's France was, in fact, undergoing the transition from Rococo to Neoclassical and the *bombé* shape was giving way to a serpentine curve. More usually, commodes were constructed on a rectilinear plan, sometimes with a slight projection at the centre, of the kind known as 'breakfront', which remained fashionable for about ten years. A modified cabriole leg, its sweep less pronounced, was eventually replaced by a straight one, of square or round section but tapered and fluted, while commodes which came down almost to floor level were given turned feet. This simplification of line did not result in any appreciable reduction in the luxury of the decoration. Ormolu mounts, although these were the first feature to be adapted to the new fashion, were still lavishly applied and of the finest quality.

Marquetry, which employed both floral and Neoclassical motifs, also remained popular. Some commodes were now fitted with doors which either concealed or took the place of drawers, and Japanese lacquer screens were ruthlessly segmented—often with little regard for their design—to provide panels for this purpose. Boulle inlay was revived and some of the commodes of this period were frank adaptations of Louis XIV prototypes. Jean-François Oeben, who had served as an apprentice under the sons of Boulle, was one of the outstanding cabinetmakers of the period. He had two distinguished pupils, Jean-François Leleu and Jean-Henri Riesener, both of whom sought to marry Oeben's widow and take over the business. Riesener was the successful suitor, and became the pre-eminent cabinetmaker of the Louis XVI period. His influence even extended to Sweden, where Georg Haupt, who had worked under Riesener in Paris, and had also spent some time in London, added his own distinctive touches to the style, with panels at the ends of his commodes that dipped into a semielliptical curve, and friezes inlaid or mounted in ormolu with a wavelike Vitruvian scroll.

ABOVE LEFT
Dutch bombé *commode veneered in walnut and decorated on the top with a shell in marquetry, the drawers fitted with the original delicate ormolu handles, 1760.*

ABOVE RIGHT
Italian commode, mid 18th century. The swell towards the top and the painted decoration are both characteristic Venetian features of the period.

OPPOSITE
Louis XVI commode in the Neoclassical style, in which the bombé *shape has given way to a more severe outline. The decoration is still lavish, with* pietre dure *panels. It was not unusual at this period for earlier pieces of furniture to be dismantled, and the more decorative portions of them to be made up into currently fashionable items.*

ABOVE
Mahogany commode based on a design in Thomas Chippendale's The Gentleman and Cabinet-maker's Director, *and possibly made in his workshops, c. 1755–1760. The bombé shape was attempted by few English or American craftsmen.*

LEFT
An American lowboy finely carved in the style of Benjamin Randolph of Philadelphia, c. 1765–1780. Though related in design to the English Chippendale school, the filling in of the kneehole with a carved feature—in this case, a swan—is much more American than English.

RIGHT
English serpentine-fronted chest of drawers of the Chippendale period, c. 1760, in mahogany. The relatively early date for a chest of this shape is indicated by the loop handles and the square bracket feet.

92

David Roentgen, the son of Abraham (see p. 56), was the most distinguished German cabinetmaker of the Neoclassical period. While retaining the parent workshops established by his father at Neuwied, he travelled abroad and set up branches in St Petersburg, Brussels and Paris. He was accepted as a member of the Paris guild of joiners and cabinetmakers in 1780. His work is especially remarkable for its very fine marquetry. Carved decoration of swags, ribbons and musical instruments, composed in a rather taut manner, characterizes other less important but very agreeable two-drawer German commodes of the period.

Polish craftsmen who worked under Roentgen at Neuwied carried his methods home with them to Warsaw, probably influencing the estate-owned workshops at Kolbuszowa (Little Poland), which produced commodes and other pieces notable for their use of exceptionally wide walnut cross-banding around areas of marquetry and parquetry.

In Britain the *bombé* shape seems either to have lacked popular appeal or to have presented too many problems for the craftsmen. A few of the most distinguished of them, including Chippendale, handled it with distinction but not much before 1770. At mid-century the rectilinear form was still preferred for the chest of drawers, and the most popular wood was mahogany, left severely plain save for its brass handles, and sometimes some restrained carving on the canted corners. The feet were usually of the bracket type, either square at the corner or fashioned into an S-shaped 'ogee' curve. A few important specimens were made at this time, which deserve the term 'commode' in the sense of being intended for use in the drawing-room rather than the bedroom. These were mounted on separate stands with cabriole legs and ball-and-claw feet. About 1750 the restrained English form of the serpentine front began to appear. Examples with a depth of four drawers are usually regarded as superior to those with only three, but as always, every article must be considered on its own individual merits.

These basic patterns of the mid-eighteenth century were followed in America, where the style was known as 'American Chippendale', but many of the chests of drawers display characteristics that clearly distinguish them from their English counterparts. A shape known as 'block front', owing something to German sources, introduces a series of gentle protrusions, often in association with boldly carved shells, which are said to have been first applied in this way by Job Townsend of Newport, Rhode Island. His family intermarried with that of

Thomas Goddard, and several members of each became highly skilled cabinetmakers.

The block-front chest was also made in Connecticut and in Boston, Massachusetts, where Benjamin Frothingham produced, about 1770, some outstanding double chests of drawers with this shaping to the lower section and a bonnet top to the upper. John Cogswell, also of Boston, was one of the relatively few Americans to master the full *bombé* form, shaping even the drawer sides to follow the contours of the carcase—a feature seen sometimes on the best Swedish examples, but seldom on other European specimens. Philadelphia boasted some fine carvers, among them Benjamin Randolph, whose lowboys followed the proportions of the French commode although their cabriole legs on ball-and-claw feet, acanthus leaves on the knees and carved C-scrolls on the apron were nearer in spirit to the English school. About 1770, as Chippendale had before him, Randolph claimed that he was working in the 'new French style'.

ABOVE
American blockfront chest of drawers in cherrywood, c. 1780, of Connecticut type, the projections surmounted by carved shells. The cabriole legs terminate in ball and claw feet—a feature that remained popular in America much later than in Britain.

BELOW
English serpentine-fronted chest of drawers of the Hepplewhite period, c. 1780, with oval plate handles and splayed feet indicative of this date.

In the second half of the eighteenth century, Holland imported such large quantities of English and French furniture that in 1771 this commerce was prohibited in order to protect the interests of the native craftsmen. These men produced their own version of the Neoclassical style, employing panels of lacquer in the oriental manner on a ground of satinwood. A type of commode peculiar to the Netherlands was one with a hinged top that could be raised to reveal a rack holding an urn for water, with a washbasin below. This was intended, not as a bedroom washstand, but as a convenience in the drawing-room for washing drinking glasses.

Painted decoration in the style of Angelica Kauffmann and Michele Angelo Pergolesi gave a mildly Italian flavour to many English commodes made during the period dominated by the architectural designs of Robert Adam. The painting sometimes covered the entire surface, but more often was confined to the decoration of a satinwood ground on cupboard commodes of semielliptical form, with three or four doors, the centre section being fitted with drawers inside. This type was also decorated with classical urns in marquetry—a style associated with the name of William Gates, of whom little is known other than that he enjoyed royal patronage between 1777 and 1781. (Very similar commodes were produced at about the same time in Scandinavia.) These commodes were intended for use in the drawing-room, while the more usual chest of drawers for bedroom use was most often executed in mahogany, square, serpentine or bow-fronted in shape with slightly splayed feet. Although ormolu was produced in Britain for lavish furniture that imitated the French style, the more usual type of handle was of brass—circular, oval, octagonal or in the form of a lion's head. Marquetry decoration employing satinwood, harewood (sycamore stained green) and other light-coloured woods is sometimes to be found on mahogany chests of the Hepplewhite and Sheraton period, but this is often an embellishment added much later, about 1900.

The Federal period in America saw the rise of New York as a source of fine furniture. This was mostly modelled on the designs of Hepplewhite and Sheraton, but executed with vigour and touches of

originality by craftsmen such as Michael Allison, Elbert Anderson, and the firm of Stover and Taylor, not forgetting the illustrious Duncan Phyfe. The Skillin brothers of Boston were carvers of great skill who produced Neoclassical statuettes in wood to surmount double chests of drawers, while the Seymours made some commodes that were semielliptical, with tops veneered in fan patterns of contrasted dark and light woods. This style continued into the early Republican period, about 1810, by which time the later phase of Neoclassicism was well established in Europe.

The Empire style, which was common to most of Europe, with minor regional variations, transformed the commode into a rectilinear carcase of great severity, resting on a flat plinth. This was relieved with bronze mounts cast in the form of laurel wreaths and a stylized form of the anthemion, with columns at the corners surmounted by sphinx heads, or simply by inlaid stringing of light wood such as box on a dark mahogany ground, or the ebony stringing on *bois clair*, such as maple or cherry, which became fashionable, especially in Austria and France, during the Biedermeier period.

ABOVE
*English washstand, c.
1870. Although the only
feature this type of article
may appear to have in
common with a French
commode of the 18th
century is a marble top,
good examples often
have splashbacks made of
ceramic tiles with some
artistic merit.*

BELOW
*Art Deco dressing chest
c. 1925. Although
furniture of the 1920's
is sometimes as vulgar as
a gangster's moll, it can
also have the charm of
the bright young thing.*

RIGHT
*French Art Nouveau
commode veneered in
walnut, designed by
Louis Majorelle. In
the hands of the Art
Nouveau designers, the
chest took on new and
surprising forms,
becoming sometimes
part of a composite
piece of furniture.*

Birch satisfied a similar preference for light-coloured wood in Russia. In Denmark the severity of the commode was often relieved with a large, rounded arch veneered with a wood in contrast to the rest of the front. The British used a brass inlay on a ground of mahogany or rosewood for commodes in the Regency style; but the chest of drawers for bedroom use—a much more typical product—continued to be made in mahogany with a flat or bowed front and knobs of brass or wood. Military chests with countersunk brass handles were made for the campaigning army officer.

As the nineteenth century advanced, the general trend internationally was for the commode to be relegated to the bedroom, and also to grow heavier in appearance. Massive columns appeared at the corners, tops became thick, feet bulbous, knobs hefty, and the quality indifferent as commercial manufacturers competed for a price-conscious market.

Some reform was effected by the Arts and Crafts and Art Nouveau movements, with August Endell in Germany and Ambrose Heal in Britain making praiseworthy attempts to rescue the chest of drawers from its plight. They lowered the height to table level and used oak and elm in place of mahogany. In the 1930's, R. W. Symonds and Robert Lutyens used flush surfaces in burr walnut, with tassel-like handles, on chests that were proportioned rather like those of the Empire period, while Serge Chermayeff adopted strict geometric shapes with horizontal wooden bars as handles, achieving dramatic effects with strongly marked veneers such as macassar ebony.

Today, the need for a chest of drawers as a separate piece of furniture has largely been eliminated by built-in units, and as a status symbol it might be assumed to have disappeared. It has not. It has merely been absorbed into a larger and even more impressive storage system.

THE BOARD AND THE CUPBOARD

The word 'table' is derived from the Latin *tabula*, meaning 'board'. At one time these terms were more or less synonymous, and even now people sit around a table at a board meeting, hoping that when it is over, there will be a drink waiting for them on the sideboard. The Romans, and the Greeks and Egyptians before them, were not in the habit of eating at a large table. They reclined on couches placed around a central area, with food and wine within easy reach on small stands. A Roman table with a circular top on three legs carved or cast in bronze to resemble those of animals was imitated in the late eighteenth century. The typical Roman rectangular table with a marble top resting on carved stone supports was a sideboard rather than a dining table, and this, too, was copied centuries later, during the Renaissance.

Such grandeur was unknown in the early Middle Ages, but the principle of a large top resting on a series of supports persisted. When it was necessary for people to crowd together within the safety of the castle walls, the entire community sat down to eat at tables which were often erected only for the duration of the meal and then taken apart. They were flat boards supported on trestles, shaped like pairs of triangles joined together at top and bottom. Later in the Middle Ages, during the Gothic period, the supports became single posts resting on a crossbar and with a parallel cross piece above on which the top rested. A more elaborate version rested on supports that reflected the influence of church architecture. The base was shaped like a square cross and from it rose four buttressed verticals set at right angles to each other.

Some splendid Italian Renaissance tables were based on the ancient Roman principle of resting the top on two or three slablike supports, elaborately carved in stone or wood to represent animals or monsters. Those made of stone, with inlaid marble tops, were closely modelled on Roman originals but their use was confined to the richest houses. Those made in wood were less faithful to the classical prototypes, but more imaginative in their use of strange figures, half animal, half human. The rather wild imagery of such Mannerist designs was kept within bounds by a powerful architectural discipline, evident in the mid-sixteenth-century designs of Jacques Androuet Ducerceau of Lyons and Hugues Sambin of Dijon, in many of which the classical column played a rôle as important as that of the human figure or the winged monster. Some French Renaissance tables had mythological figures carved to form end supports, but between them ran

German table, made at Augsburg in 1626 by Hans Georg Hertel and Lucas Kilian, employing a pietre dure top of earlier date, probably composed by Cosima Castrucci in Prague, c. 1580. A rich variety of materials have been used. The woods include ebony, pearwood and walnut; the metals, gold, silver, bronze; the semi-precious stones, agate, jasper, lapis lazuli.

ABOVE
English oak side table,
15th century, supported
on columns, the
mouldings reflecting the
influence of sacred
architecture on furniture
of this period.
BELOW
English oak drawleaf
table c. 1600, the legs
typical of the English
Renaissance style, the
extending top derived
from the Netherlands.

a secondary support of rounded arches resting on turned pillars, while some of Ducerceau's designs for tables eliminated the sculptured figures entirely and concentrated instead on Corinthian columns.

The traditional Spanish table, often made of chestnut, on splayed end supports braced to the underside of the top with struts of wrought iron, had appeared before 1600. The frame of the trestles was sometimes made from turned members, sometimes of flat lengths of timber with their edges scalloped. This type of table has been made in Spain ever since, which makes the precise dating of individual specimens extremely difficult.

Another type of table which began to be made about 1600, this time in Germany, was that with

X-shaped end supports, which gradually replaced the simpler trestle version, and has continued in production until the present. The 'X' is sometimes curved in a manner that was familiar in ancient civilizations. A cruder version, in which the cross members of the supports are straight, is still found in many parts of Europe and not so very long ago used to be a standard piece of equipment in many a country inn. It has a cross member joining the end supports, which may be pegged or, in later versions, screwed into position. The wood is often a combination, with oak, pine, elm and various fruitwoods being the most common.

A table capable of extension, and clearly aimed at catering for family life in a domestic setting, was

OPPOSITE BELOW
Two dropleaf tables,
that on the left English
and clearly the prototype
for the second, which is
American in the Queen
Anne style, early 18th
century.

invited in the Netherlands about 1600. This had a framed construction of four boldly turned legs, joined together by a frieze above and stretchers below. The top rested on this frame, but was not fixed. Concealed beneath it at each end was a leaf that could be drawn out, supported on sliding bearers. When both leaves were fully extended, the main part of the top dropped automatically into position. The mechanism is so simple and effective that it is still used by modern manufacturers of dining-room tables.

This type of table arrived in Britain from the Netherlands soon afterwards, and immediately enjoyed great popularity. The elaborate Italian and French Renaissance tables with sculptured supports do not seem to have been imitated to any great extent in sixteenth-century England, whose inhabitants evidently preferred the Dutch form with four, six or even eight legs of bulbous shape. The name 'refectory' is commonly applied to this long, narrow shape, which implies a monastic origin; but the best of such tables, in the bold style of the English Renaissance, are more in the spirit of the buccaneer than the bishop. Simpler versions were made with legs of slimmer proportions, turned or

left square, until the mid-eighteenth century—often with a matching set of stools or benches that could be tipped at an angle and stowed under the table when not in use.

Folding tables were made in great variety. A type popular in Italy and South Germany from about 1600 had shaped slab ends connected by an understretcher, rounded drop leaves supported by swinging legs or iron brackets, and a deep drawer at one end. The 'fold-over' gateleg table was more usual in France, the Low Countries and Britain from about 1610 to 1650. This formed a half-round side table when closed, opening to a full circle with the leaf supported by a swinging 'gate'. A similar table had a top which was octagonal when open. The type is known as a 'credence' table, but there is little evidence that it was ever intended specifically for use during the Communion service. It was replaced in popularity at mid-century by the conventional gateleg with two drop leaves supported on legs turned to a bobbin, baluster or spiral shape. Exceptionally large examples had two gates supporting each leaf. Benjamin Franklin refers to one in his autobiography, saying that he remembers 'thirteen sitting at one time at his table'.

ABOVE LEFT
American gateleg table in walnut and cherrywood, the well-turned legs terminating in the type of foot known as 'Spanish' or 'Braganza'. This table is believed to have once belonged to Benjamin Franklin and to be the one referred to in his autobiography. Tables of this type were popular in England, Holland and America, from about 1650 to 1720.

ABOVE RIGHT
Italian walnut table, late 16th century, the drop-leaves supported on iron brackets. The type was also made in Southern Germany.

The gateleg was immensely popular in the Netherlands, Britain and America, the usual woods being oak, walnut or fruitwood, worked in the solid. The design continued to be made well into the eighteenth century. Until about 1700 the tops were usually pegged to the frames with dowel pins; after that date they were screwed. An interesting American variation, made between 1700 and 1750, was the 'butterfly', so called because its leaves were supported on hinged brackets shaped like the wings of a butterfly, pivoted between the frieze and the understretcher. It stood on four well splayed, turned legs, and was oval when erected.

In America and Britain, a drop-leaf table, rectangular or oval when open, that dispensed with the extra gates by allowing the right-hand cabriole leg to swing out and support the leaf was produced shortly after 1700 in walnut, and from about 1725 in mahogany. The tops were usually in the solid wood, not veneered. Veneers were employed on the tops and friezes of tables less subject to damage, such as those made for playing cards, which were made on the fold-over principle, the interior surfaces being lined with baize or, as a special refinement, needlework, with a shallow space left at each corner for candlesticks. Like the drop-leaf, the gaming table was supported by one or two hinged legs. The fashion for tea drinking caused many tea tables to be made on the same lines as the gaming table but with polished surfaces inside. In American versions cherry is a frequent alternative to walnut or mahogany. Examples made in Philadelphia tend to be more robust than those of New England.

The Pembroke table, named after the Countess who first suggested it, had short flaps supported on hinged brackets. In the 1770's, when the design first became popular, the top when open was usually oval, square or with serpentine shaping on the sides. There are some fairly plain mahogany specimens, but a number of such tables were made in satinwood with marquetry or painted decoration. After the 1790's a turned centre column with four splayed feet gradually replaced the tapered legs.

The later decades of the century saw the production of some fine tables in the Neoclassical style in every major European centre of production. Reduction of imports from abroad stimulated the Amsterdam guild to new efforts, the long tradition of fine marquetry work being maintained at a very

high standard by such craftsmen as Andries Bongen. Dutch furniture of this period is often stamped with the arms of the city, flanked by the letters 'J.G.' for 'Joseph's Guild'. The Portuguese, during the reign of Queen Maria (1777–1816), made elaborate games tables with tops finely inlaid with ivory for games such as chess and backgammon. In the reign of Louis XVI the French made toilet tables with lift-up tops, the interiors fitted with compartments to hold cosmetics, and work ables, constructed on much the same lines but fitted out to accommodate the needlewoman's requisites. Towards the end of the eighteenth century these were made with end supports in place of the usual four legs. The British

ABOVE
American cherrywood table in the Queen Anne style, which survived in America until the mid 18th century.

BELOW
American card table of West Indian satinwood made by Duncan Phyfe of New York, early 19th century.

BELOW LEFT
English table with square dropleaves, the legs terminating in pad feet, mid 18th century.

OPPOSITE
Walnut gaming table on cabriole legs, carved with shells on the knees *and terminating in ball and claw feet; English, first quarter of the 18th century.*

and the Americans made fitted dressing tables with rising mirrors under the lift-up top, lowboys with oval or shield-shaped toilet mirrors, and washstands, either square or made with bow fronts to fit in a corner. These have a circular hole cut in the top to receive the washbowl, and the modern user would be ill advised to cover the whole with a new top that cannot easily be removed. To do so would reduce the value considerably.

Tripod tables were made in large numbers both in Britain and America throughout the eighteenth century in every grade from workaday oak to splendid creations in mahogany. In the better-quality articles, the tops are either circular with carved pie-crust edges or octagonal with delicately fretted galleries, their centre stems finely turned to baluster shapes, their feet adapted to the cabriole curve and terminating in pad, ball-and-claw or hoof forms. When the Rococo style gave way to the Neoclassical, the tripod table—especially in its smaller version, the 'wine table'—acquired a more slender column, a thinner top that was often oval, and feet that swept away from the column in a downward curve.

Rectangular or oval breakfast tables were also constructed on the principle of the centre column with splayed feet. The top was in one piece but hinged to a block at the top of the column so that it could be tipped to a vertical position, making it easy to take through narrow doorways—breakfast tending at that time to be literally a movable feast. The 'drum' table had a similar base; the circular top had drawers fitted in the frieze, and was made to revolve.

The sofa table was often equipped with a very similar central support, but the type with end supports, plain or lyre-shaped, usually commands a higher price today. Such tables were fashionable in Britain, Scandinavia and parts of America between 1800 and 1830, Duncan Phyfe and the New York school being responsible for some distinguished examples. In Denmark a similar design was used as a dining table.

In France, until the late eighteenth century, comparatively little attention was paid to the dining table, a simple board covered with a good cloth being considered adequate in even the most luxurious homes. About 1790 a circular type of table on a very severe central pedestal set a fashion that quickly spread all over Europe.

The most usual dining table in Britain and America in the last quarter of the eighteenth century consisted of three detachable units, each of which could be used independently. The central section had rectangular drop leaves to which half-round ends could be added, and extra leaves that could be inserted as required. The favourite wood was mahogany, and the legs were usually square tapered. From about 1800 onwards these were replaced with pedestal supports formed from turned columns and splayed feet. The firm of Gillow of Lancaster patented a table in 1800 with a system of sliding bearers which enabled it to be extended at will, and another, designed by Richard Brown and patented a few years later, used a concertina-like hinged action that made it a relatively small side table when closed but expanded to seat about 18 people. Late in the nineteenth century came the table on four heavy legs that could be extended simply by turning a handle.

RIGHT
American candlestand on tripod base, c. 1790, the stem carved in the manner of Samuel McIntire of Salem (1757–1811), one of the most distinguished craftsmen of the Federal period.
FAR RIGHT
Inlaid mahogany corner washstand in the Heppelwhite style, but made in New Brunswick c. 1790 by Matthew Egerton and bearing his trade label—a rare feature.

LEFT
Circular table on central pedestal, the top inlaid with brass—a style of decoration that became fashionable in the early 19th century. It was a specialized craft centred in St Martin's Lane in London. This example is probably the work of an immigrant Frenchman, Louis le Gaigneur, who set up a factory about 1815 in Edgware Road where he revived the Boulle technique of inlaying brass into tortoiseshell.
RIGHT
Sofa table on end supports, the feet sweeping out in a sabre-shaped curve. English, early 19th century. The type was also popular in Denmark and America.

The most interesting tables made during the last years of the century were those in the Art Nouveau style. Emile Gallé and Victor Horta both designed tables in which the legs resembled the stems of plants and seemed almost to be growing from the floor. Horta contrived large dining tables based on this idea without allowing the sinuous line to run riot. Gallé would seem to have been happier with smaller tables in which the tops, as well as the legs, are based on natural, growing forms.

The twentieth century has produced a whole new range of tables, some scrupulously functional, with glass tops on metal stands; some, especially those in the Art Deco style, striving after novel effects by stretching to their limits the possibilities of sheer surfaces and curving shapes afforded by plywood. The need for a low table to be used in conjunction with modern seating led to the creation of the coffee table, and all kinds of adaptations of traditional forms, as well as genuine inventiveness, were employed in the process. One of the greatest modern advances has been in the use of new finishes to wood, such as surfacing it with polyurethane, to protect it from spilled drinks and hot dishes. Tables moulded from plastics meet the same requirement and, because there are no problems of jointing, can be made in a variety of new shapes, which would have delighted the designer of a couple of hundred years ago who had to contend with wood's lack of plasticity.

The console table The console or architectural side table in late seventeenth-century Italy had a top of Florentine mosaic work—incredibly detailed designs being laid out with minute pieces of coloured stone, set in plaster on a slab of stone. This rested on a Baroque stand which would probably be a piece of sculpture in wood depicting the human figure, in the style of Brustolon. In France slightly more restrained versions of such tables were designed by Jean le Pautre. In Germany, Augsburg and Nuremberg were the chief centres of architectural design and of furniture of this kind, which was intended to occupy a particular place. The number of rooms in a German house was a matter of strict protocol by the end of the seventeenth century, and a family's status was implicit in the degree of importance permitted in such dominant features as the side table and centre table. The peak in such design was reached with tables that were overlaid in solid silver. Some massive console tables of sculptural form, with matching pier glasses above them, were an integral part of William Kent's houses in Britain in the 1730's.

The sideboard America followed the English mid-eighteenth-century practice of having a fairly plain mahogany serving table, at either end of which a pedestal cupboard surmounted by an urn-shaped knife box or water tank, would be placed as a free-standing piece. The credit for the invention of the sideboard with a cupboard built in at each end, or with deep drawers, standing on square tapered or slimly turned legs, should probably go to George Hepplewhite. Modified versions of this design were popular in America during the Federal period, the whole of the carcase normally being occupied with cupboard and drawer space, whereas the English version more often had a kneehole at the centre. American decoration on such sideboards was also more restrained, and usually confined to simple stringing in light woods on the mahogany ground; some designs, however, were finely carved on the leg, notably those by Samuel Field McIntire of Salem, produced early in the nineteenth century. The most prolific use of marquetry decoration was on the Scottish sideboards of that period.

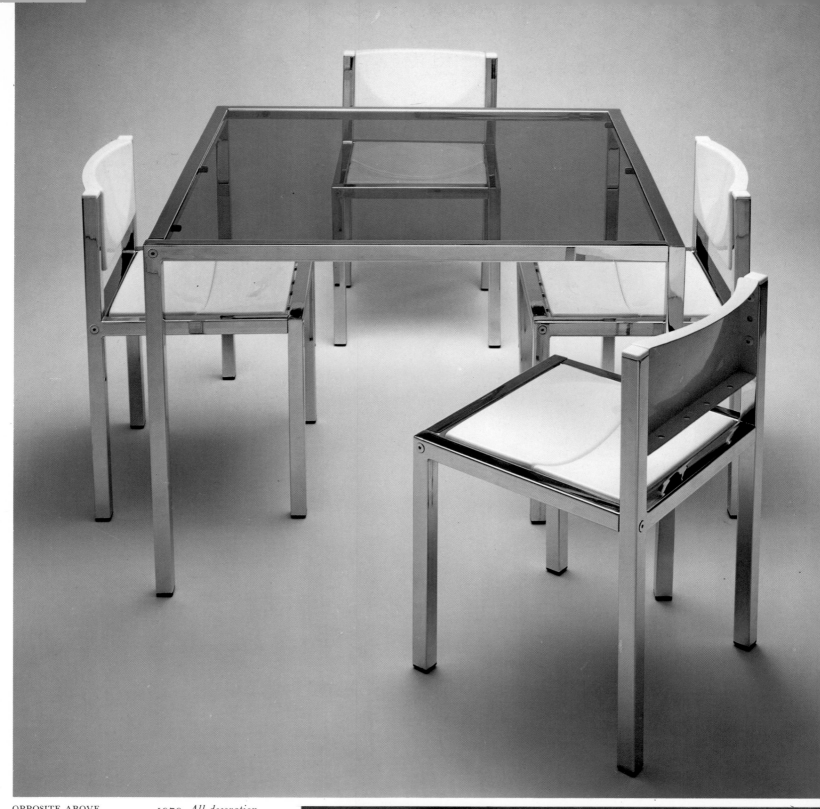

OPPOSITE ABOVE
American serpentine-fronted sideboard made by John Aitken of Philadelphia and acquired by George Washington for the banqueting hall at Mount Vernon in 1797.

OPPOSITE BELOW
Russian table on central pedestal, early 19th century, with circular top of malachite—a favourite Russian material—and ormolu mounts.

ABOVE
English glass-topped table on a metal stand, c. 1970. *All decoration having been excluded, this must succeed or fail on the strength of its proportions and fitness for purpose.*

RIGHT
Eighteenth-century Italian console table. Carved and gilt, this Venetian example is typical of the special place occupied by the console table everywhere —a carefully calculated position related to the architecture, and little concerned with functionalism. It is simply a prestige symbol.

After about 1810 many sideboards were constructed on the principle of two pedestal cupboards joined by a flat top. In the space between the pedestals stood a wine cooler or 'cellarette' of sarcophagus shape. This type prevailed in America, Britain and the Teutonic countries until about 1840. Towards the middle of the century it became ever more monumental in design, with a vast mirror above, often flanked by brackets and surmounted by an architectural pediment reaching almost to the ceiling. Heavy swags of fruit or dead game birds were favourite devices for the carved decoration applied to the cupboard doors. The Arts and Crafts Movement influenced design by reducing the overall height to a more human scale, but the sideboard remained essentially a tall piece of furniture, with cupboards flanking or entirely replacing the mirror back. Strap hinges of copper attached the doors to the carcase, and the upper cupboards were glazed with 'leaded lights'—imitated from ecclesiastical stained-glass windows—in the more commercial products; some, however, were painted by competent artists in the Pre-Raphaelite style.

About 1900 August Endell in Germany used the splayed-end shape of early Chinese furniture for sideboards, as he had with chests of drawers. They were solidly constructed and free of all superfluous decoration. A few years later, Eugène Vallin, one of the designers working at Nancy in France, adapted the high, mirror-backed sideboard to the Art Nouveau style, using boldly curved supports, like the branches of a tree, for the shelf above. In Holland, after World War I, Gerrit Rietveld was responsible for some revolutionary designs for sideboards with no superstructure, which consisted simply of storage compartments mounted on frames with all their construction visible.

Though there has since been a reaction in favour of concealed joints and a smooth exterior, it was this kind of basic approach that succeeded in breaking with the nineteenth-century tradition of massive proportions and excessive decoration, and prepared the way for the present-day sideboard—especially the Scandinavian type, with its emphasis on the horizontal line, which owes something, too, to the simplicity of the best work of the late eighteenth century.

The dresser Originally the French *dressoir* was a board placed at the side of the room on trestles—a sideboard on which drinking cups were placed. This was the 'cup board'. Because its primary object was the display of wealth and the assertion of rank, it became the practice to construct the *dressoir* in several stages or tiers, their number being decided according to social standing.

The French walnut *dressoir* or buffet illustrated below is in the style of Hugues Sambin, and is elaborately carved, the upper stage being enclosed by doors and supported below by winged monsters. In the English 'court cupboard' the space above was not enclosed but the triple-tiered construction was essentially similar. Compared with the sophisticated carving of the French example, which was probably a product of Dijon in the later sixteenth century, the rather flat carving of the scrolls on the English piece appears a little naive and provincial.

BELOW
English court cupboard, late 16th century, exhibiting French Mannerist influence in the carving of the supports, but very English in the rendering of the bands of scrollwork.

BELOW RIGHT
Console table formed as a classical head flanked by husks and acanthus leaves, mounted on an architectural plinth, designed by William Kent for Chiswick House, in the 1730's.

109

Relatively few English court cupboards had the supports formed like monsters, the more usual feature being bulbous turnings. Early in the seventeenth century, the spaces began to be enclosed by cupboards. The lower turnings were the first to disappear, but those above remained for a while, the ends of the cupboard being canted to allow for them. In late examples, made about 1780, all that is left of the turning is a pendant knob at each end of the cornice—often seen in the Welsh versions.

One exception is the American version, the 'press cupboard', made in Massachusetts about 1700, which sometimes retained the bulbous turnings both above and below. Its doors were decorated with carving and split turnery.

In some areas of the world the dresser resembled this press cupboard in many ways. In others it reverted for a time to being a side table, fitted with drawers. Versions of this are to be found in many countries, standing on turned legs with three or four drawers set in the frieze. In Portugal in the second half of the seventeenth century, the legs were very boldly turned with large protuberances towards the top, while in Holland, Britain and America the legs were slimmer and the drawer fronts were decorated with mouldings.

The dresser would be 'dressed' with decorative metalwork and pottery, and a rack of shelves was often hung above it for the display of Delft or other earthenware, known, for obvious reasons, as the 'Delft rack'. About 1700 this rack began to be attached to the dresser—probably for added stability. In this way, what is popularly known as a Welsh dresser came into being, but in fact the dresser and rack style is by no means confined to Wales, or even to Britain. In the eighteenth and nineteenth centuries, nearly every home in Europe and America boasted a dresser of some kind, either

RIGHT
Oak cupboard dresser, North Wales or border counties, the base completely enclosed with cupboards and drawers, and small cupboards embodied in the rack above; fitted with the original brass loop handles and standing on curved bracket feet of the type known as 'ogee', c. 1770. The South Wales dresser has an open potboard in the lower stage.

RIGHT
English dresser c. 1900 in the Art Nouveau style. The splayed shape of the carcass owes something to the influence of Chinese furniture. The metal fittings are typical of the period.

free-standing or built-in, but after about 1840 it was regarded as little more than a kitchen fitment.

Almost every region can make its claim to a type of dresser that has some distinguishing feature, for example: the open pot-board below the drawers in South Wales; the domed top to the rack in Holland; the base with cupboards and drawers between them in northern Britain; an asymmetrical arrangement of cupboards, drawers and shelves in Switzerland; elegant cabriole legs in the border counties of England and Wales.

The armoire The French cupboard, like the English, gradually came to be fully enclosed, though it was made in two sections and called an *armoire à deux corps*—a two-part cupboard. Before 1600 the carving was usually rich but disciplined, and the upper stage was a little smaller than the

lower, making the two-part construction obvious. After 1600, however, the carving tended to cover the whole surface and the upper section was fully as wide as the lower, giving the piece the impression of being constructed as a whole. Eventually, appearance became reality, and the *armoire à deux corps* became the armoire—a full-length wardrobe. In fact, this single unit has existed since the Middle Ages as the church sacristy cupboard and in some areas, particularly the north of Germany, had been known as a piece of domestic furniture well before the French type developed. Enclosed cupboards in two stages were also popular in sixteenth-century Germany, the upper stages having caryatid supports to the cornices and vivid inlaid decoration on the panels of the doors.

In Italy, too, as the seventeenth century advanced, the *cassone* gradually gave way in popularity to the

BELOW
French Renaissance cupboard in two stages (armoire-à-deux-corps) *carved in typical Mannerist style, mid 16th century.*

ABOVE LEFT
*Detail of French
armoire, second half of
the 17th century,
decorated with metal
inlay in a tortoiseshell
veneer, in the manner of
André-Charles Boulle.*
ABOVE RIGHT
*French provincial oak
armoire, c. 1750–1780.
The shaping of the door
panels corresponded to the
panelling of the walls of
the room. Similar
wardrobes were made in
the Low Countries and
Germany.*

armoire, constructed as either two units or one massive wardrobe. Its design was architectural, with spiral columns or classical pilasters supporting the projecting cornice. Decoration was carving in the Renaissance style, and the inlay known as intarsia, which was remarkable for the optical illusion of perspective created in the designs of buildings and landscapes.

In the second half of the seventeenth century the French armoire came to be decorated with brass inlay on a tortoiseshell ground, in the manner of Boulle. This was expensive work that could be afforded only by the rich. More modest, but still very handsome, armoires were made in oak, walnut or fruitwood. In the eighteenth century they had doors carved to match the panelling of rooms in the Louis XV style—a type that continued to be made in provincial areas until the nineteenth century.

By the middle of the eighteenth century a rather different form of wardrobe had evolved in other countries. In England, Holland and Sweden, especially, this took the form of a cupboard with doors placed on a base which was essentially a chest of drawers. In Britain it was known as a 'gentleman's wardrobe', and was fitted in the upper

stage with sliding trays (clothes usually being laid flat, not hung). The shape was almost always rectilinear in the English version, but Dutch and Swedish specimens have *bombé* bases. The standard test piece for a craftsman seeking entry into the Stockholm guild was a wardrobe of this type.

The wardrobe became even more massive during the nineteenth century, acquiring full-length mirrors attached to the outside of the doors. The reformists of the Arts and Crafts and Art Nouveau movements tended to add decorative details in their own idioms rather than to deal with the basic problem of the oversized wardrobe. It was not until the early 1930's that a radical approach was made, reducing the scale to manageable proportions and removing the heavy projecting mouldings that had made this piece of furniture a mothballed temple in the previous century. Gradually, the unit principle gained in popularity, and although the traditional wardrobe is still produced as an independent piece of furniture, or as part of a bedroom suite, it has become much more reticent. In many homes, indeed, it has now been replaced by the built-in wardrobe and become part of the actual building.

ABOVE
*Pair of wardrobes
designed by Charles
Rennie Mackintosh
c. 1900, with a chair by
the same designer placed
between them. This
grouping emphasizes the
vital importance of seeing
certain pieces of furniture
in their architectural
setting.*

RIGHT
*Fitted wardrobe and
dressing table in light
oak. English, c. 1970.
The traditional concept
of a bedroom suite,
established in the 19th
century and originally
comprising wardrobe,
dressing-table, washstand
and chest of drawers, is
abandoned in favour of
an overall design
embracing hanging space,
drawer space and working
top with mirror.*

LEFT
*Louis XIV cabinet on
stand, decorated with
metal inlay in a
tortoiseshell ground in
the manner of
André-Charles Boulle;
second half of the 17th
century.*
OPPOSITE
*Cabinet on stand
c. 1700 painted with*
chinoiseries *in the style
of Gerard Dagly, a
native of Spa, who
specialized in this kind
of decoration and worked
for Frederick the Great of
Prussia.*

BELOW
*Cabinet of drawers on
sculptural stand,
elaborately decorated with
marquetry, the interior
painted with a view of
Versailles. Made at the
Royal French Furniture
Factory and presented to
Charles II of England
by Louis XIV of France,
second half of the 17th
century.*

The cabinet The cabinet, in its many forms, is
perhaps the clearest example of a piece of furniture
designed as a luxury item in its own right and as a
container for smaller valuables. It is only too easy
to despise such things as nonfunctional, but without
this urge to display status symbols our heritage of
furniture would be very drab indeed.

The cabinet illustrated on page 29 is French,
made of solid walnut and dating from the second
half of the sixteenth century. It employs classical
columns and is carved with a representation of a
nude figure, in the Mannerist style of Ducerceau. It
is a highly sophisticated version of the *dressoir* of the
same period (see page 108).

In the seventeenth century this form developed into
the cabinet on stand—a highly fashionable article all
over Europe—consisting of an upper stage with
many small drawers, either exposed or enclosed by
doors, mounted on a stand. Decoration was lavished
on the surfaces of the drawer fronts, on the doors,
where these were used, and on the legs of the stand.
In Italy, the drawer fronts were inlaid with Florentine mosaic or encrusted with *pietre dure*. In Spain
the *papeleira* had drawers veneered in ivory or
tortoiseshell. In Portugal the *contador* was fitted with
heavily moulded, projecting drawer fronts and
rested on a stand with a deep apron, fretted and
carved, between boldly turned legs. In Holland and
Britain, after 1660, the drawers of cabinets were
finely veneered in walnut and decorated with
marquetry, and enclosed by doors similarly treated;
the legs were spiral or turned to the inverted cup
shape. France produced some extremely rich
cabinets decorated with Boullework, mounted on
elaborately carved legs. In the Netherlands, Antwerp
was a celebrated centre for magnificent Baroque
cabinets, the drawer fronts carefully painted on
marble, the stands carved with the figures of
negroes, muses or caryatids.

Trade was now developing with China and
Japan, and one of the most popular seventeenth-
century imports was the lacquer cabinet. This
conformed in many ways to the European type,
having drawers within enclosed doors, the whole
richly decorated in lacquer. These cabinets usually
arrived without stands, and were mounted on
arrival onto Baroque supports, which were richly
carved and gilded but had little or no stylistic
resemblance to the oriental character of the objects
they supported. The first such cabinets arrived
from the Far East about 1600, and by 1616 an
Englishman, William Smith, was at work in Rome,
copying them. This soon became a popular industry
with centres in Venice, London, Spa (near Liège),
Berlin and at the Gobelins factory outside Paris. The
Portuguese made a thriving trade out of importing
the authentic article from the East, as well as copies
from England. They also made their own reproductions and sold these, as well as the English
copies and oriental originals, very successfully in
Paris. In the eighteenth century lacquering became
popular in America, and Boston was the chief
centre for the work. In 1688 two Englishmen,
John Stalker and George Parker, published *A Trea-
tise on Japanning and Varnishing*, which gives detailed
instructions for using shellac, a distillation made
from the secretions of bark lice, which was the
substitute used in Europe for true oriental lacquer.
Many cabinets were decorated by amateurs in
England, and their quality varies greatly. A cheap
version made in Venice was *lacca povera* (poor man's
lacquer), made by fixing prints to a coloured
surface. The best lacquer copies were made by the
Dutch.

Another immensely popular novelty from the
Orient was porcelain, which began to be made in
Europe shortly after 1700 and soon created a

demand for display cabinets which were either open or enclosed by glazed doors. In some countries the passion for the display of porcelain in the Chinese style led to the creation of large cabinets surmounted by pagoda-shaped tops.

In France cabinets were made in the Rococo style, usually with veneered doors mounted with plaques of Sèvres porcelain. The vast majority of cabinets in the Louis XV style, with shaped glass doors, that are seen on the market today were in fact made in the nineteenth century. They have panels painted in the *vernis Martin* style, with Watteau and Boucher subjects.

The Neoclassical period produced some very elegant cabinets with glazed doors. In America the designs of Sheraton were adapted by Nehemiah Adams of Salem, who created a personal style typified by a kneehole in the lower stage and very delicate treatment of the glazing bars of the case. Corner cabinets were produced in all grades, some with glazed doors above, some entirely of wood, some full-length, some meant to hang from the wall. There is a popular fallacy that all 'genuine' corner cabinets should have 13 panes of glass in the door. The French *encoignure* was a dwarf corner cupboard standing on the floor, with a wooden door, frequently decorated in marquetry and usually with a marble top. Similar types were made in Germany, Holland

and Scandinavia. The Scandinavian countries also produced some attractive farmhouse corner cupboards with incised and painted decoration.

Early in the nineteenth century small cabinets on stands, reminiscent of the seventeenth-century type, were decorated with very careful 'penwork' drawings of classical, oriental and floral motifs. Dwarf cabinets, standing on very short feet, were made in France and elsewhere with doors inlaid with brass on rosewood or on tortoiseshell. This revival of the Boulle technique continued well into the 1860's. Some dwarf cabinets have a door of this type at the centre and a bowed glass door at each end. The door may be inlaid with marquetry or Boullework, or embellished with a porcelain plaque. Because of its popularity in Italy, the type is now known as a 'credenza'.

The decorative possibilities offered by the cabinet made it a favourite object among the members of the Arts and Crafts and Art Nouveau movements. In England cabinets designed by William Burges and painted by Pre-Raphaelite artists reflect the love of medieval colour. The French adapted the sweeping lines of the Rococo in creating cabinets for the display of particular admired objects, such as Gallé glass. In Russia a style midway between Arts and Crafts and Art Nouveau brought a Neoclassical flavour, absent in most of the Western European work, to cabinets with arched fronts. In Germany Endell decorated the doors of cabinets with wavy lines inspired by his observation of seaweed growing under water. Early in the twentieth century, Heal imparted an original touch to cabinets of basically eighteenth-century style, using oak in its natural

colour, while Frank Brangwyn designed some highly decorative specimens with doors faced in carved and painted *gesso* (plaster).

The Art Deco style is seen at its best in the elegant cabinets of severe outline, softened by curving feet, in the manner of the French designer Ruhlmann, and at its most bizarre in 'modernist' cocktail cabinets of chunky form, lavishly veneered on the outside and lined inside with mirror glass. Contemporary cabinets are generally severe in outline, and good use is now being made of sliding glass doors, which offer the maximum opportunity for viewing the contents.

Dwarf cabinet decorated with marquetry, of the type now known as a 'credenza', typical of a basically Louis XVI type revived in France in the 1860's and much copied.
BELOW
Satinwood cabinet with painted panels, designed by E. W. Godwin c. 1877.

Mid 18th-century English oak corner cupboard, the interior with 'umbrella' top and curved back, for the display of porcelain.

The bookcase In medieval times, before the invention of printing, books were laboriously written by hand, and because they were so precious, they were locked away in chests or displayed individually, as works of art, on wall brackets or chained to reading stands. Early records prove that during the Renaissance, when the number of books to be housed increased, cupboards and shelves were simply built into the walls of a room set aside as a library. Free-standing bookcases were hardly known until the second half of the seventeenth century, and in some European countries they never replaced the built-in type in popularity. Even when they came to be made, during the eighteenth century, as separate pieces of furniture independent of the house architecture, they usually remained architectural in conception and many were actually modelled on classical buildings, complete with plinth, columns, frieze, cornice and pediment. The same was true of the bureau bookcase.

The 'breakfront' bookcase, favoured in Britain and America, had a centre portion projecting a couple of inches forward, relieving the monotony of the front. This usually had four glazed doors above and either drawers or cupboards, or a combination of both, below. Early in the nineteenth century a dwarf bookcase made its appearance, and a number of open shelves to hang on the wall or stand on the floor were also made—often painted black, with the edges of the shelves relieved with gilt.

Massive constructions, their doors reinforced with brass *grilles* to protect the books, continued to be made, and the architectural element grew continually stronger during the later phase of Neoclassicism, when Roman, Etruscan, Greek and Egyptian ornament was applied in a rather ponderous fashion. During the Gothic revival that continued to influence library furniture throughout the nineteenth century, the large bookcase looked less like a Roman temple and more like a cathedral. This flavour was only slightly reduced by the Arts and Crafts Movement, but the Art Nouveau designers—who were highly conscious of books as beautiful things, illustrated by some of their own artists—lightened the whole structure by the use of curving lines and by lifting it off the ground with legs. The bookcase still remained a large and slightly forbidding piece of furniture until the present century, when designers came to realize that books needed to be accessible—easy both to see and to reach. Many unit systems were invented, so that a library could be extended as desired, and there is now a wide range of shelving available which can be added to or rearranged at will, in which the framework is often made of metal.

The desk In medieval times the desk had been an article with a sloping top on which manuscripts and books were rested. Sometimes it was mounted on a stand, but more often simply placed on a table, or on the writer's knee.

The Renaissance in Germany produced small writing tables, which were much in demand in an age of steadily increasing literacy. They were often ornately carved, with a pendant turning below each corner of the frieze, and some have cleverly concealed drawers. The idea of a secret drawer has always had a romantic appeal, and some form of it is to be found in writing desks of most periods. Some of these early German tables had rounded leaves which could be folded down.

The Spanish *vargueno* (writing cabinet) first appeared in the sixteenth century and has remained a characteristic Spanish type ever since. The upper stage was of boxlike construction, fitted with many small drawers and a writing leaf which was hinged

OPPOSITE ABOVE
Late 17th-century French writing table or bureau Mazarin *with Boulle decoration of brass inlay in a ground of tortoiseshell.*
OPPOSITE BELOW LEFT
Spanish vargueño—*a writing cabinet on a base fitted with drawers, their fronts displaying Moorish influence in the decoration; 17th century.*
OPPOSITE BELOW RIGHT
French portable table with a small leaf extended for writing, decorated with marqueterie-à-la-reine *on the frieze. Attributed to Charles Topino, c. 1770, this table is in the transitional phase from the Louis XV to the Louis XVI style.*

at the lower front edge, so that it was in the vertical position when closed. The stand was sometimes an architectural construction of turned legs, or a carcase fitted with doors or deep drawers. The decoration was almost always very elaborate. Spanish-Moorish designs were inlaid in silver in the style known as 'plateresque'. Fine wrought ironwork was mounted on a background of tooled leather or rich velvet, while engraved or painted plaques of ivory were often used on the drawer fronts.

The French *bureau Mazarin* of the Louis XIV period, named after his principal minister, was a flat-topped writing table standing on eight legs. In the 1660's these were vertical, square and tapering with bold protrusions near the top, but towards the end of the century they were more often scroll-shaped. The bureau has three drawers at each side—bow-fronted in the later versions—and one above the kneehole at the centre. The usual decoration was Boullework. The type was closely imitated in other countries, notably by Gerreit Jensen, a Dutch craftsman who emigrated to London in the late seventeenth century. Many writing tables of simpler form, with only one drawer in the frieze and standing on spiral legs, were made in Holland and Britain at this time. Their tops were often masterly exercises in marquetry, with vases of flowers being a favourite subject, sometimes with the addition of the owner's coat of arms and monogram. Antwerp was an important centre for marquetry work, the products of Peter de Loose and Michel Verbiest reaching a particularly high level of excellence.

The French discarded the heavy preponderance of drawers and the mass of legs embodied in the *bureau Mazarin* and replaced it early in the Louis XV period with the *bureau plat*. In this the four sides of the flat top were shaped into gentle, serpentine curves harmonizing with the sweep of the cabriole legs. Either the top was leathered within a wide cross-banding of veneer or the whole surface was decorated in marquetry. This design underwent a further change during the Louis XVI period, when the legs became straight and tapering, and the top rectangular. Kingwood, purplewood, ebony, mahogany and many other beautiful veneers were used. Ormolu of the finest quality was mounted in continuous, fretted bands along the frieze and drawer fronts. Sometimes it would be still further enriched with Sèvres porcelain plaques. An adaptation of this basic form was the cylinder-top desk, so-called because of its cylindrical cover that enclosed the

top. The utmost trouble was expended on magnificent specimens of this type, which was the forerunner of the popular roll-top desk that came to be made commercially in the nineteenth century. Smaller versions were made for women, in both the French and English styles. In England, the tambour top replaced the solid cylinder with a flexible cover composed of strips of wood glued onto a linen backing. Another desk intended mainly for women was a small writing table with a flat top surmounted by a superstructure of small drawers—known as the *bonheur-du-jour*.

Oval and kidney-shaped desks became popular about 1800. Giovanni Socchi, a Florentine cabinet-maker working in the French Empire style, made some ingenious desks with extending tops and concealed chairs which slid out when required. This kind of mechanical conjuring trick is really more typical of German craftsmen of the period, one of whom, Peter Kinzing, produced some highly contrived furniture at the Neuwied workshops. A favourite device of his was a set of drawers which rose from the flat top of a desk at the touch of a button.

TOP
French bureau-plat, *a typical flat-topped writing table of the Louis XV period, mid 18th century. The eight legs of the* bureau-Mazarin *have given way to four, of elegant cabriole shape, and decoration is mainly confined to finely chiselled ormolu mounts.*
ABOVE
Italian writing table, signed and dated 'P. Piffetti, Turin, 1741'. Typical of this craftsman's skill in elaborate marquetry, it may have been designed by Filippo Juvarra, Sicilian architect to the House of Savoy.

Catherine the Great of Russia imported furniture from France, Germany and Britain to be copied by native craftsmen, most of whom were serfs. They seem, however, to have enjoyed a fair amount of freedom in interpreting foreign styles. Russian writing tables in the Neoclassical style were embellished with ormolu mounts of great magnificence, whose design was more in the spirit of the Baroque.

A type of desk which was based, in principle, on the Spanish *vargueno*, developed in several countries after 1700. This had a fall front which was vertical when in the closed position, and rested on a lower stage of drawers. Behind the fall front was a fitment of small drawers, and there was often a concealed drawer in the cornice above. This type was made in finely figured walnut veneers, particularly in Holland, Britain and Germany, during the early eighteenth century. In France during the Louis XVI period it was made in one piece, instead of two, and the fall was often enriched with a plaque of royal Sèvres porcelain, set in an ormolu frame, which was only visible when the desk was closed. Dutch examples were richly decorated with marquetry, the entire surface sometimes being covered with designs of flowers, birds and urns. In Germany and Scandinavia the type remained in fashion during the Biedermeier period in the early nineteenth century. Mahogany and birch were favourite woods, and the top acquired an architectural superstructure of rising steps—a feature usually seen only on specimens of northern European origin.

A small, flat-topped desk with drawers on each side of a kneehole, in which a cupboard was recessed, was fashionable in Britain when walnut was the principal wood in the early eighteenth century, and continued to be made even when mahogany had superseded it. In America the kneehole was given more elaborate treatment by shaping, or 'blocking', the drawer fronts.

The desk with a fall front that rests on the carcase at an angle when in the closed position—the English 'bureau'—was made in many countries and was descended from the medieval desk with sloping top. Originally, this sloping surface was hinged at

ABOVE
Louis XVI bureau cylindre by J. H. Riesener (1734–1806) —one of several of this type made by him following his completion of that begun for Louis XV, left unfinished by Oeben who died in 1763.

RIGHT
Writing table attributed to David Roentgen, the most distinguished German cabinet maker of the 18th century, who became a maître-ébéniste of the Paris guild in 1780.

its upper edge to give access to the interior. Late in the seventeenth century it began to be hinged on the lower edge, so that it could be lowered and rested on two supports that slid out, which were known as 'lopers'. The interior was fitted with small drawers, and the arrangement of these became simpler rather than more complex as the type gradually developed in the eighteenth century. Often they have a small cupboard set in the middle of the range of drawers, flanked by a pair of columns that conceal secret drawers. This kind of desk at first rested on a separate stand, composed of turned legs in the late seventeenth century, and cabriole legs in the early eighteenth century, with one or two drawers set in the frame. While this type on legs continued to be made well into the Neoclassical period, with legs that changed shape correspondingly, a more substantial carcase developed, which was really a chest of drawers with a desk above.

When a cupboard or cabinet was placed on top of this, it became the article variously known as a 'secretary cabinet', 'bureau bookcase' or 'bureau cabinet'. The American secretary desk, in its earlier form, is often distinguished by a bonnet top and the decorative use of a large shell. In its later phase, during the Federal period, it was a most gracious piece of furniture, the best examples of which, such as those made in Philadelphia, employ very little carving and rely on ovals of pale veneer set into a background of mahogany to achieve their effect.

The Dutch type often had a *bombé* base and double-dome top, with mirror glass in the doors. The German version was perhaps the most ambitious, with very elaborate serpentine shaping on the lower stage and magnificent marquetry work on the doors above. Japanning in imitation of oriental lacquer was a favourite form of decoration on this type of article in Germany, Holland, Portugal, Britain, America and Italy too, during the earlier part of the eighteenth century. The English and American preference, however, was for a more severe appearance. Using good quality timber, the English produced 'bureau bookcases' in oak, walnut and mahogany, first with wood doors, then mirror glass,

BELOW
Russian fall-front secretaire made of Karelian birch in the Neoclassical style of the Tsar Alexander I period (1801–1825). The stepped top anticipates a similar feature in Austrian Biedermeier secretaires.

LEFT
Secretary desk, the base on ogee bracket feet, the upper stage with characteristic mid 18th century American bonnet top.

RIGHT
American blockfront kneehole desk, carved with shells in the style particularly associated with the Townsend and Goddard families of Newport, Rhode Island, third quarter of the 18th century.

finally clear glass divided into small panes by glazing bars which, as well as achieving a good decorative effect, overcame the problem of making large sheets of glass free of imperfections.

The English library desk was really a larger version of the kneehole, with a flat top resting on a pair of pedestals fitted with drawers. It was meant to stand in the centre of a room and was finished on all four sides. The side facing the visitor was often given a deceptive appearance by simulated drawer fronts. Some particularly fine library desks were made by Chippendale in the second half of the eighteenth century and by his son during the early years of the nineteenth. Plainer versions with practical drawers on both sides continued to be made and used as partners' desks in businesses throughout the nineteenth century.

In the 1890's, C. F. A. Voysey designed some fallfront desks that were raised on legs with cupboards above, and the doors sometimes decorated with pictorial designs in metal. At about the same time, the Dutch architect, Henri van de Velde, working in a highly disciplined version of Art Nouveau, was responsible for several truly magnificent flat-topped desks with sweeping curves that embraced open shelves as well as drawers on each side of the kneehole. These paved the way for the more ambitious type of modern 'executive' desk which, though eminently functional, is also as much a status symbol for the business man of today as the *bureau plat* ever was for the eighteenth-century aristocrat.

Conclusion One of the most successful manufacturers of modern office furniture has confessed that when he put his best executive desks on the market at competitive, economic prices, he encountered serious sales resistance. The men who were to sit at them felt their dignity demanded something

ABOVE LEFT
Partners' desk in the Sheraton style, veneered in satinwood. English, late 18th century. This type is the precursor of the modern executive's desk.
LEFT
Austrian oak secretaire with marquetry

decoration in various woods on the fall front depicting a sporting scene with huntsmen and hounds.

BELOW
Mahogany military secretaire chest bearing the maker's label of Hill and Millard, London, mid 19th century.

more costly. The manufacturer increased his selling prices substantially, and the sales then rocketed.

Designers of today may no longer imitate the splendour of royal palaces, preferring to find their inspiration in the streamlined environment of the luxury hotel, the air terminal and even the cabin and flightdeck of the aeroplane itself; but the need to flatter the owner's ego seems as much in evidence now as it ever has been. Mass-production methods employing an abundance of man-made materials and eliminating fussy ornamentation might surely result in really good furniture being available at a low cost. Many manufacturers strive with commendable success to achieve this aim but there is also, sad to say, a very large quantity of furniture being made which, although it may appear relatively cheap, seldom compares favourably with the simple products that were made by country craftsmen for peasant communities before the onset of the Industrial Revolution. Today anything individually designed and custom built to a high standard is usually only for the affluent.

If this seems a depressing note on which to conclude, some solace may be found in acceptance of the idea of furniture as a status symbol. Although this may not appear, at first glance, a very admirable quality, and in spite of the profusion of vulgar monstrosities it has at times brought into being, it has to be recognized as a vital and indispensable factor in the creation of beauty in the home. The disciples of functionalism may repudiate the principle with indignation, pointing to revolutionary changes in attitudes and methods of manufacture in a technological age; but designers of furniture will almost certainly continue to aim as in the past, at the creation of things in the possession of which their owners may take an understandable pride.

LEFT
Lady's writing desk in the French Art Nouveau style, bearing the branded signature of Louis Majorelle of Nancy, c. 1900.

BELOW
Rosewood-topped desk on chromium-plated stand, 1972. This austere design satisfies the principle laid down by Le Corbusier of furniture as 'equipment' in a 'machine for living' and, by softening the hard effect of the chromium with a rosewood top, goes some way towards satisfying the need for beauty in furniture.

Index

Page numbers in *italic* refer to illustrations; page numbers in **bold** refer to captions.

Acknowledgments

Antique Collectors' Club 84 below
Apsley House 106 below
Avon Antiques 85 above
Musée Royale de l' Afrique Centrale, Tervuren 38
David Bagott Design Ltd. 43 below
Historisches Museum, Basel 80 below
Bavaria Verlag 34 below, 78, 79 above, 98–99, back of jacket (centre right)
Bethnal Green Museum 70 right, 71 left and above right, 96 above right, 106
right, 119 above
Museum of Fine Arts, Boston 92 below (gift of Maxim Karolik), 94 (gift of
Miss Martha C. Codman, the M. & M. Karolik Collection), 95 left (M. & M.
Karolik Collection), 102 below right (M. & M. Karolik Collection)
British Museum 26
Brooklyn Museum 82, 86 left, 102 above
Duke of Buccleuch & Queensberry 114 below
Ca' Rezzonico, Venice 2–3, 10 below, 30 above and below, 31, 55 below, 90 right,
107 below, 121 below
Schloss Charlottenburg 115
Château de Compiègne 95 below right
Christies 16–17, 29 above left, 56 right, 85 below, 87 below right, 88, 93 below
left and right, 108 below, 109 below left, 117 above, 120 below left
Museum of the City of New York 67 above
Collectors' Guide 15 above right, 23 below, 36, 53, 83 above, 120 above and
below left
Cooper-Bridgeman Library 50 above, 63 above, 106 below, 122 below, 123 above
right
Courtauld Galleries 75
Craig & Tarlton Inc., Raleigh, N.C. 105 above right, 108 above, 123 left
Crispin 60 below left, 61
Graham Dark 56 left, 80 centre, 81 below
Michel Dumez-Onof 29 below, 100 above, 101 above right
English Manor Antiques 100 below left (photo Raymond Fortt)
Egyptian National Museum 27
Werner Forman 18–19, 23 above, 26, 27, 38, 44, 91, 114 above, back of jacket
(top left)
Fratelli Fabbri, Milan 30 below
Furman Collection, New York 44
Geffrye Museum 70 left
Mark Gerson 118 above left
Keith Gibson 113 above
Ginsburg & Levy Inc. 64 below (photo Helga Studio)
Giraudon 46, 95 below right, jacket back flap
Hamlyn Publishing Group 89 below
W. & R. Harvey & Co. 25
Heal & Son Limited 97 above
Bevis Hillier 35 both (photo Julian Neaman), 72 centre, 96 below (photo
Bulloz)
Michael Holford 22, 58
Homer, Price & Partners 124 above
Angelo Hornak 2–3, 7, 10 below, 15 above and below left, 30 above, 31, 40 above
right, 47 above right, 51 above, 54 below left, 55 below, 59 right, 60 above,
66 above, 71 below, 75, 90 right, 96 above left, 102 below left, 107 below,
121 below, 122 above, front of jacket (left), back of jacket (centre left)
India Office Library & Records, London 23 above
Instituto Vendite, Giudiziarie, Florence 50 below
Edward James Foundation 72 below
Tobias Jellinek 28, 29 above right, 49 left
John Keil, London 104
King & Chasemore 36
Bob Loosemore 21 above, 24 above

Luton Hoo 123 above right
Mallets 9 below, 10 above, 15 below right, 21 above (photo Bob Loosemoore),
24 (photo Bob Loosemoore), 54 above, 60 above, 65 left, 68 below right,
118 below, 120 above, 121 above, 122 below
Metropolitan Museum of Art, New York back of jacket (top left)
Mount Vernon Ladies Association Union 106 above
Musée des Arts Decoratifs, Paris 40 above left, 46, 57, 111 right, jacket back flap
Museum of Modern Art, New York 37 above (Purchase mfr. Isokon Furniture
Co., England), 37 below (Gift of the mfr., Herman Miller Furniture
Company, U.S.A.), 69 (Gift of Cafe Nicholson), 72 top right (Gift of Herbert
Bayer), 73 above (Gift of Thonet Industries, Inc.), 73 centre (Gift of the mfr.,
Herman Miller Furniture Company, U.S.A.)
Münich Residence 66 below, back of jacket (bottom)
National Trust (Clandon Park) 116 above
Nima 40 above left, 111 right
Philadelphia Museum of Art 92 above
Philp and Sons, Cardiff 9 above, 14, 33 both, 42 above, 55 above, 62, 63 below,
68 below left, 79 below, 83 below, 87 above right, 90 left, 95 above right,
·111 above left, 112 right, 116 below, 117 below left, 120 below right, 124
below left and right
Phoebus Picture Library 57, 67 below, 107 below right, 115
M. Raeburn 1
George Rainbird Ltd. 114 below (photo Tom Scott)
Rijksmuseum, Amsterdam 52 left, 77 below
Roger-Viollet 8 (Collection Viollet), 41, 77 above
Room for Living 97 below
Collection Rothschild 91, 114 above
Royal Academy of Arts 117 below right (Handley Read Collection)
Royal Ontario Museum, Canada 118 above right
Israel Sack Inc., N.Y.C. 101 above left
H. & R. Sandor Inc., New Jersey 87 left, 123 below right
Shaker Museum, Sabbath Bay, Maine 59 left
Silvester, Warwick 105 below
Sothebys 17, 48 left, 72 above left, 76, 81 above
Sothebys Belgravia 72 centre left, 125 above
Spacefitta 113 below
Shirley Plantation, Virginia 40 above right
Spink & Son Ltd. 20 all, 21 below, 24 below right, 84 above
Stadtmuseum, Munich 67 below, back of jacket (centre right)
Staples & Co. Ltd. 119 below
David Stockwell Inc., Wilmington, Delaware 101 below, 105 above left, 109 above
left and right
Tiroler Volks Kunstmuseum, Innsbruck 39
V. & A. 6 (photo A. C. Cooper), 7, 22, 32, 43 above, 45, 47 above left and
below, 48 right, 50 above, 51 below left, 58, 103, 112 left, 118 above left,
122 below, front of jacket (left)
Vono 73 below left, 107 above, front of jacket (below right), back of jacket (top
right)
Waddesdon Manor 122 above, back of jacket (centre left)
John S. Walton Inc. 93 above (photo Helga Studio)
Geoffrey Warren 111 below left
O. F. Wilson 24 below left, 40 below, 64 above, 65 right, 68 above, 89 above
Henry Francis Dupont Winterthur Museum 49 above right, 60 below right,
86 right, jacket front flap
Joseph Ziolo, Paris 43 (photo Jean Candelier), 66 below and back of jacket
(bottom) (photo Jean Candelier), 103 (photo Jean Candelier)

The illustration on the front of the jacket (above right) is the Great Hall,
Rockingham Castle (courtesy of Commander Michael Saunders-Watson; photo J. Whitaker); that on the back of the
jacket (top left) is a Roman bed. The endpapers are from Thomas Chippendale's *The Gentleman and
Cabinet-maker's Director.*

I. Chippendale inv.t et del

Publish'd according to